Gunpowder,
treason and plot

The gruesome story of Guy Fawkes

© Day One Publications 2005
First printed 2005

ISBN 1–903087–96–1

9 781903 087961 >
ISBN 1–903087–96–1

British Library Cataloguing in Publication Data available

Published by Day One Publications
Ryelands Road, Leominster, HR6 8NZ
☎ 01568 613 740 FAX 01568 611 473
email—sales@dayone.co.uk
web site—www.dayone.co.uk
North American—e-mail—sales@dayonebookstore.com
North American—web site—www.dayonebookstore.com

Designed by Steve Devane and printed by Gutenberg Press, Malta

This book is dedicated to:
Professor Julian Evans, John Jacobs, Michael Newton, Paul Susans,
Dr Philip West, Denis Cocks, Timothy Pinchen,
Christopher Warwick and Stephen Warwick
Elders, Deacons, wise men and very good friends

Contents

I am grateful to many people for their help in the production of this volume. The leadership team and members of the Butts Church in Alton, not only for sitting through a *Gunpowder Plot* presentation, but also for their great patience and many encouragements.

To Lester and Sylvia Brewer for valuable information regarding Ightham Mote. This helped in clarifying a number of issues regarding Dorothy Selby.

And where would I have been without the indefatigable John Roberts of Day One, with his boundless energy, enthusiasm and encouragement? To all the staff at Day One, my sincere thanks for their expertise and practical help in turning a mere manuscript into this book.

I am grateful to Rev. Dr Kenneth Brownell for his kindness in writing the foreword. He has been a good friend over many years and a great travelling companion on different preaching tours.

Last, but not least, my thanks to my wife, Amanda, for preparing the illustrations, and to her and our son, Luke, for their tolerance towards me in the writing process.

As is the common lot with all authors, I take responsibility for what I have written and if any sources have not been acknowledged, this matter will be rectified in any subsequent printing.

Clive Anderson
August 2005

Foreword

This is a timely book. I write this foreword just a week after the 7 July bombings in London when religiously motivated terror struck at the heart of the nation. But this wasn't the first time terror had been planned ...

In 1605, there was a plot to blow up the Palace of Westminster when King James I and many of the leading people of the land would be assembled for the opening of Parliament. Happily the plot failed, but, had it not, Britain today would very likely be a completely different nation. In this gripping book, Clive Anderson tells the story of the Gunpowder Plot which is mainly known today (if it is at all) by the annual celebration of Bonfire Night on 5 November.

Here is everything one could want in a story—plots, conspiracy, terror, spies, religion, politics, torture and much more. However, Clive not only tells us what happened, but also puts the plot in its broad historical and theological context. Here is an excellent introduction to Reformation history and theology through the lens of this historical episode that may be bait with which to catch the interest of a younger Christian.

Judicious comments scattered throughout the book enhance the contemporary relevance of the plot to our own day as we now experience religiously-motivated terrorism. For today, we are facing the problem our ancestors faced in the seventeenth century—that is, the presence of a significant number of people who want to impose a different religion on the nation and some who want to do so by violent means. This book sheds some light from the past into our present travail. Read it for pleasure, but read it also for wisdom.

Rev. Dr Kenneth Brownell
Senior Pastor, The East London Tabernacle,
London, England

Remember, remember the fifth of November
Gunpowder, treason and plot.
I see no reason why gunpowder treason
Should ever be forgot.
Guy Fawkes, Guy Fawkes,
'Twas his intent
To blow up the King and the Parliament,
Three score barrels of powder below
Poor old England to overthrow.
By God's providence he was catched
With a dark lantern and burning match.

Verse from an unknown seventeenth-century writer

The Houses of Parliament

Glossary of terms

Appellant	Person who compromises between the state and Roman Catholicism
Confession	Heard in secret by a priest who will then forgive the sins that have been confessed
Dissimulation	Secret adherence to a faith or belief
Equivocation	Speaking the truth to oneself while lying to another person
Excommunication	To exclude from the communion and privileges of the Church
Heretic	Those who were deemed to go against official Church teaching and interpretation
Intention	Any wickedness may be committed provided the 'Intention' is directed to a good end
Jesuit	A member of the Society of Jesus founded by Ignatius Loyola and Francis Xavier in 1534
Martyr	A person who dies for his or her beliefs
Pope	Head of the Roman Catholic Church and considered by Catholics to be the successor of the apostle Peter and Christ's representative on Earth
Poursuivants	Government agents who searched for hidden priests
Protestants	Those who protested against the Church of Rome and its practices
Puritan	English Protestants who wanted to 'purify' the Church and society
Recusant	Any person who refused to attend Protestant services
Roman Catholics	Those who adhere to the rites and rituals of the Church of Rome

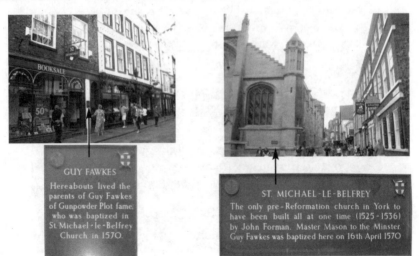

Guy Fawkes in York

The big bang

'Let love and faithfulness never leave you; bind them around your neck, write them on the tablet of you heart.' Proverbs 3:3

'Clarence, Ninth Earl of Emsworth, is dressed and ready to go to London to attend the opening of Parliament, but the unwilling Peer of the realm does not want to leave; so reluctantly, he potters off, thinking as so many others had thought before him, that the ideal way of opening Parliament would be to put a bomb under it and press the button.'[1]

Strange how little has changed with the passing of the years. It has been said of Guy Fawkes that he was a rare case of someone entering Parliament with honest intentions!

Treason

Increasingly, though, apart from fireworks displays every year and the odd programme on television, generally rather little thought is given to The Powder Treason (the first name ever given to this incident) and its implications, which, if it had been successful, undoubtedly would have dramatically changed not only British history but also that of the world. At the very least, England would probably have been invaded, and Spanish would have become the dominant language of the British Isles.

It is the day rather than the year that is generally known, although the reasons for The Gunpowder Plot and its cause and failure are forgotten in the annals of history. Yet it is a significant event in English history and should be remembered, as the first part of the famous rhyme puts it:

'Remember, remember the fifth of November
Gunpowder, treason and plot.
I see no reason why gunpowder treason
Should ever be forgot.'

The year of this momentous event was AD 1605, and The Gunpowder Plot had a profound effect at that time and was for many years considered to be worth commemorating as a significant event in the history of Parliament and England. In the past, the Anglican Church has commemorated this day, with orders drawn up for special services to enable many to show their thankfulness to God for his rich mercy towards them in preservation and blessing.

Preaching on the Bible text, Isaiah 54:17, on Sunday morning 5 November 1854 at New Park Street Chapel, Southwark, in London, the twenty-year-old Baptist, Charles Haddon Spurgeon, said:

This is the fifth of November, a day notable in English history. The events which transpired on it ought never to be forgotten. On this memorable day, the Catholics, foiled in all their schemes for crushing our glorious Protestantism, devised a plot horrible and diabolical enough to render them for ever hateful amongst upright men. The vast Armada of Spain, on which they had relied, had been by the breath of God scattered and given to destruction; and now the cowardly traitors attempted, by the foulest means, the end of which they could not accomplish by open warfare. Under the Houses of Parliament the deadly powder was concealed which they hoped would be the death-blow to both houses, and so annihilate the power of Protestantism; but God looked from heaven, he confounded their knavish tricks, he laid their secrets bare, and discovered their treachery. Hallelujah to the King eternal, immortal, invisible, who guarded us, and guards us still from the devices of Rome and hell! Praise to his name, we are free from the Pope of Rome, to whom Britons never will be slaves.

While for our princes they prepare,
In caverns deep a burning snare,
He shot from heaven a piercing ray
And the dark treachery brought to day.[2]

What is a Christian?

Underlying the plot was the question that has vexed people down the centuries: 'What is a Christian?'

The only way any person can find the right answer is through God and what he has revealed in the Bible. The Bible opens by stating that God is holy and eternal, and that he created everything that exists, and the height of his creation were men and women, beings made in his image. However, they disobeyed him by listening to Satan, the devil, who appeared in the form of a serpent, and followed his ways. Sin is the name the Bible uses to describe this disobedience to a holy God. As a result, human beings fell from the favour that they enjoyed in the Garden of Eden and were banished from that perfect place. Death entered the world as a direct consequence. Yet a great promise was made to them in the Garden before they left, that God would not abandon the human race, and would send a Saviour who would undo the sin of Adam.

As the biblical record continues, this great developing theme unfolds through the long and rich tapestry of the Old Testament, until the time that the deliverer, the Messiah promised of old, appears on earth. Remarkably, he is not only a perfect man, but is also perfectly God, a unique person. He is the God-man whom the Bible calls Jesus; this supernatural coming together of one who is both fully God and fully man is a great and profound mystery. Jesus came to live a perfect life, and then died the perfect death as God's chosen sacrifice, shedding his life-blood on a cross at Calvary. Three days later he rose again, triumphant from death, to show that his sacrifice had paid the price of sin for his people. He then ascended back into heaven where he reigns as King, and will come again to judge the world and bring in the eternal destinies for all that have ever lived.

Before he returns, people have to respond to him, recognizing that he died once, for all sin. They have to repent—that is, say sorry and turn away—from their sins and receive the free gift of having him in their lives as Lord and Saviour. Then, by the power of God the Holy Spirit, they need to live the rest of their lives for God's glory.

According to the Bible, there is only one way to God—through Jesus Christ alone. All other ways do not lead to peace and eternal life. But Satan does not like what God has done; in his malevolent way, he tries to confuse simple matters and so, for example, tradition becomes mixed up with truth so that it is difficult for people to see the way they should go. This is what lay at the root of the Gunpowder Plot; it is not just a quaint or engaging story from England's history; rather, it was a serious attempt to pervert the truth and blind people to the only way to God.

This plot, along with its main 'celebrity', Guy Fawkes, is not, as one writer has dismissively described it, 'His failed mission [which] provided English children with their equivalent of Halloween, Guy Fawkes Night, when bonfires are lit and fireworks set off amid a party atmosphere.'[3] It is much more serious and far reaching that that description allows.

A trip back in time

Peering through the mists of time, we may gain a glimpse of that momentous year of 1605 and look into the lives and homes of people that were illuminated by candle or rush light, with earth floors strewn with vegetation and with no sanitation or running water. Even the privileged few living in castles, palaces or manor houses would be amazed to see how the average western dwelling is equipped today, with appliances that we now consider essential but which would then have been beyond people's wildest dreams.

A brief (if inadequate) visit will be made into a world where life was often cruel, with plagues and epidemics bringing devastating consequences, where pain generally went unrelieved, and the majority were faced with great uncertainties about life itself. The normal person was, therefore, weighed down with fear and doubt both within and without, and the people looked to leaders, both secular and spiritual, to alleviate their daily grind.

Despite the passage of time, the great principles and truths at stake then are still relevant today, for God's Word is timeless and speaks powerfully to each generation. Many years, later referring to the events of that day in 1605, the Puritan pastor and author John Flavel (1628–1691) said in his book *Tidings from Rome or England's Alarm*:

And O God would make our honourable representatives in Parliament still vigilant to observe, and zealous to oppose the motions of the enemy. We bless the Lord for what you have already done, in detecting them so far; but we cannot think our danger over, whilst they swarm in such numbers among us.

O be as zealous for the Protestant interest as they are against it; if they dare to smite with the fist of wickedness, we hope you will not be afraid to smite them with the sword of justice. Remember what a matchless salvation was once given to our English Parliament, I mean from the powder-plot, that Catholic villainy, as one aptly calls it; such a deliverance as ages past cannot parallel in any history.

Had it not been recorded in our own annals, posterity would never believe it. They have indeed studiously endeavoured, in their late bold remonstrance, to hide from your eyes the goodness of God in that deliverance, that so by forgetting his goodness, they might bury in silence their own wickedness; we hope none of your acting's against the enemy will be stained with lukewarmness; if justice be sprinkled with a favourable hand, like a few drops of water upon a fire, we doubt instead, of quenching, it will rather increase the flame. Rome is a nettle, the more gently it is handled, the more it stings. My lords and gentlemen, here is an enemy that deserves your hottest zeal, and greatest vigilance, much better than honest loyal Nonconformists, who plead with God night and day on your behalf.[4]

To some this may appear an extravagant statement, but in a modern world where politicians are always warning about the threat posed by terrorists, this four-hundred-year-old plot does sound strangely familiar.

The Gunpowder Treason Conspirators

Robert Catesby

Thomas Wintour

John (Jack) Wright

Thomas Percy

Guy Fawkes

Robert Keyes

Thomas Bates

John Grant

Christopher Wright

Robert Wintour

Sir Everard Digby

Ambrose Rookwood

Francis Tresham

Conspirators unmasked

'Do not withhold good from those who deserve it, when it is in your power to act.' Proverbs 3:27

Between 1500 and 1650, London's population may have increased eightfold. 'London was for the sixteenth century vagabond what the greenwood had been for the medieval outlaw—an anonymous refuge. There was more casual labour in London than anywhere else, there was more charity, and there were better prospects for earning a dishonest living. In the late sixteenth and early seventeenth centuries men suddenly became aware of the existence of a criminal underworld.'[1]

'Kill them all!'

Criminals chose the Houses of Parliament, in the City of Westminster, to be the scene of liberation and new order. Against this backdrop, the players were selected and motivated to act. It is not totally clear what the inducements to action the conspirators received, beyond the utopian dream of bringing in a new order by going back to an England that no longer existed, and one in which they expected themselves to play a significant role. It was claimed that one of them, Robert Keyes (who was not a rich man) joined the conspiracy with the prospect of gaining wealth and riches in the new Roman Catholic state that was expected to be ushered in.

Invariably, though, the people who take part in and win a battle lose out to their political masters, who tend to cheer on from the sidelines, encouraging greater effort, while minimizing the dangers to their own lives. Then, when the fight has been fought and the battle won, they move in like vultures to clean up. Those who plan and scheme are not normally the ones who place their lives on the line and end up at the sharp end of the action; rather, they move themselves to a place of safety.

Robert (sometimes Robin) Catesby, was the instigator of the Powder Treason. It was his intention to make the young daughter of King James, Elizabeth, the new queen. To enable this plan to be fulfilled, Sir Everard Digby was to kidnap Princess Elizabeth from Coombe Abbey, and, with this strong bargaining tool in their possession, the plotters would be in a position to dictate terms. But just who were the men behind this daring and risky proposal, and what were they like?

Know your enemy

Whenever a terrorist atrocity takes place, the first thing many want to know is, 'Who has done this thing?' Those who were involved in the plot of 1605 made up a fascinating group, and the way that they came together was not only by design but also through expediency.

ROBERT CATESBY

Robert Catesby—the acknowledged leader of the plot, was just over six feet tall, well built and handsome. This, along with his renowned charm, made him cut a dashing and imposing figure. His family had a long and interesting history: for many years, they had desired to be in power and at various times wielded it in a significant way. The family name has gone down in history because of a little rhyme that had been composed almost 140 years previously during the misnamed Wars of the Roses.

'The Cat the Rat and Lovell the Dog all ruled England under the Hog.'

Along with Richard Ratcliffe and Francis Lovell, Sir William Catesby was one of the main supporters of King Richard III during his brief reign from 1483 to 1485. Ratcliffe was the Rat, Catesby was the Cat, Lovell's family crest included a dog in it, and King Richard's badge was a hog or boar. So it was that the Cat, the Rat and Lovell the Dog all ruled England under the Hog.

After the defeat and death of King Richard at Redemore plain (better known as the battle of Bosworth), Sir William Catesby was executed. Yet this did not stop the family in their quest for power and fame, for later on Robert Catesby's father also lacked long-term political judgement and had backed the wrong side, causing him to be imprisoned for years because of his Roman Catholic faith. These things helped to build up resentment, and, when James I became King of England, the hopes of many families like the Catesbys were built up and they expected a golden age to dawn for them.

But when it did not happen, Robert Catesby said, 'The nature of the disease required so sharp a remedy.'

Catesby was an intelligent man and had been at Gloucester Hall (Worcester College) in Oxford for a short time but he left without taking a degree in order to avoid taking the Oath of Supremacy (an oath recognizing the reigning monarch as the head of the Church of England). It seems likely that he attended the Seminary College of Douai (famous for the Roman Catholic version of the Bible) then located at Rheims. This seminary was for the training of clergy, whose ranks he may have aspired to join. Interestingly, one of the textbooks used there dealt with the subject of casuistry, the employment of moral theology to particular cases. It dealt with the circumstances that might excuse a normally forbidden course of action. Could this teaching have influenced Catesby's moral framework with regard to the Powder Treason?

THOMAS WINTOUR

In stark contrast with Catesby, Tom Wintour was short and stocky, a clever man who was fluent in Spanish and French. He had fought with the English army in the Netherlands against Spain, and had also seen action in France.

He was the younger brother of Robert Wintour, but he displayed different qualities from him; Robert was considered to be a follower, whereas Thomas was a leader.

JOHN (JACK) WRIGHT

Jack Wright was one of Robert Catesby's best friends, and, like him, was tall and well built. He was considered to be courageous and strong, although inclined to be slow of speech, yet he was someone who could be trusted to keep a secret. He was the older brother of Christopher, and came from a staunchly Roman Catholic family. Along with Christopher, Guy Fawkes and Oswald Greenway (Tesimond), he attended the free school of St Peter's in York, known as 'Le Horse fayre'. His parents, Robert and Ursula Wright, suffered imprisonment in Hull for fourteen years for their Catholicism. One of their daughters, Martha, married Thomas Percy, a fellow conspirator.

John and his wife, Dorothy, endured harassment from the authorities and they appear a number of times on the recusancy roles for their profession of faith to Rome.

Along with Robert Catesby, Jack Wright had formed part of the retinue of Robert Devereux, the Earl of Essex, and, after the failure of a plot against Elizabeth I, he spent time imprisoned in solitary confinement. Catesby highly esteemed him and so he became the third to be initiated into the Powder Treason, probably in May 1604. He, along with Thomas Wintour, was given the task of informing Guy Fawkes of the plot. Although he was an active participant in all that took place, his other activities are unclear.

THOMAS PERCY

Thomas Percy was a middle-aged man at the time of the plot, and was described as being tall with stooping shoulders, having a great beard grizzled with white and near-white hair. He was the great-grandson of the fourth Earl of Northumberland, and some speculate that he may have been illegitimate. He came from a long and distinguished line that included Henry Hotspur as one of his descendants.

In 1591, he married Martha Wright, the sister of two of the other conspirators, Christopher and John. It was reported that he was a bigamist with two wives, one in the north and one in the south of the country, but that is mere speculation, as it could have been the same woman who was seen in different places. At times, he could be a bit of a wild man, and, as he had great strength, he was not a man to be trifled with.

GUY FAWKES

Fawkes was born in Stonegate, York, and christened in St Michael le Belfry. Like Catesby, he was tall and strong, but had thick brown hair and a stylish beard. He was a military man who had considerable fame among many soldiers, having seen service in the Netherlands fighting for the Roman Catholics against the Protestants. He was recruited by Catesby because he was an explosives expert and, crucially, had been out of England for a long time, so was an unknown quantity to the English authorities in general and to Robert Cecil's spies in particular.

Without doubt, Guy Fawkes was the most famous of the plotters because he was the one who was caught ready to ignite the gunpowder.

ROBERT KEYES

Keyes was a tall, red-bearded man whose virtue and valour meant he would be a reliable and dependable member of the team, and he was a good swordsman. He was the son of a rector from Stavely in North Derbyshire.

Keyes had been brought up a Protestant, but had become a Jesuit convert before joining the plot in October 1604. Compared to others in the conspiracy, he was not a wealthy man, and may well have joined because of the prospect of wealth and riches in a new Catholic state. At his trial, he claimed that he had tasted persecution for his faith and thought the lesser of two evils was to die rather than live in the midst of so much tyranny.

He was given the task of looking after Robert Catesby's Lambeth home where the gunpowder would be stored, before it was to be transferred over the River Thames to Westminster.

THOMAS BATES

Bates was born at Lapworth and became a long-standing retainer of the Catesby family. Although a servant, he was highly thought of, for he had his own servant and his own armour. When required, he indulged in cattle dealing for Catesby, who came to trust him as someone who was completely loyal and reliable.

He became drawn into the plot when he was in London in December 1604 with his master. Catesby's suspicions were aroused and he became convinced that somehow Bates had become acquainted with what was being planned. So Bates was summoned to Catesby's lodgings at Puddle Wharf, were he was questioned in the presence of Thomas Wintour. Satisfied with his answers, they both agreed to bring him into the conspiracy and they made him take the oath of secrecy, which was then sealed by the sacrament of the Mass.

Bates proved to be a useful addition to the plotters, for his position in society meant that he would arouse little suspicion when driving wagons carrying the equipment they would need to use.

JOHN GRANT

John Grant came from an old and established family in the county of Warwickshire.

He appears to have been included in the plot by February 1605, when he joined his brother-in-law, Robert Wintour, at a meeting with Robert Catesby and Thomas Percy at an Oxford Inn called *The Catherine Wheel*. They were made to swear an oath binding them to secrecy before Catesby gave them details of the plot.

He was Lord of the Manor of Norbrook, which was located a few miles north of Shakespeare's birthplace, Stratford-upon-Avon. The house was meant to be one in a chain in the Midlands of England that was to form a strong base for the rebellion that would come after the Houses of Parliament had been blown up. He was also charged with the capture of large war horses from the stables of nearby Warwick Castle; these animals would be needed for those who would join in the general uprising after Parliament had been destroyed.

Grant was described as being 'melancholy' and 'taciturn', but, when roused, he could be as fierce as a lion.

CHRISTOPHER WRIGHT

Younger brother of fellow conspirator John, he was another who, like Catesby, was tall and strong. (It is interesting that they did not seem to want to employ small insignificant men who would not stand out in the crowd.) He joined the plot on 25 March 1605, ten months after the original meeting of the five in the Strand.

Christopher (or Kit as he was sometimes called) was considered to be a good Catholic, but, of equal importance, he was a good fighter and would be invaluable if the going became tough.

ROBERT WINTOUR

He was the eldest son of George and Jane Wintour, and the elder brother of Thomas, and, when his father died in 1594, he inherited the greater part of the estate. He married Gertrude Talbot, whose father was heir to the earldom of Shrewsbury, and, therefore, one of the richest landowners in the Midlands. Like his younger brother, he joined in the plot on 25 March 1605.

SIR EVERARD DIGBY

Digby came from a family which had ancient roots, and it may be that his family had tendencies towards Roman Catholicism, but, if so, they managed to avoid suspicion. He was a strong and well-built young man, handsome and popular, and was considered to be the embodiment of all the qualities required by a dashing young courtier. In another time and place, he may have been considered suitable to play the part of James Bond, for he was an excellent musician, horseman and swordsman.

He appeared to live an untroubled and seemingly Protestant life, which was reinforced when he married Mary Mulsho, a daughter from a staunchly Protestant family. He experienced marital bliss and described his wife as 'the best wife that ever man enjoyed'. A change came, however, in 1599 when he was introduced by a neighbour to the Jesuit priest, Father John Gerard. Everard Digby suffered a breakdown in health and was attended to by Gerard, and, at his lowest point physically, Digby was received into the Church of Rome. Secrecy surrounded their friendship, but Gerard likened their relationship to that of blood brothers.

He was knighted by King James at Belvoir Castle on 23 April 1603, and so became Sir Everard, but, along with others, he became disillusioned with the promises of the king towards Catholics, for the promises seemed to vanish into thin air.

He was one of the last to be enrolled into the plot, and it seems it was as much for his wealth as for his ability that Catesby was attracted to him. It may have been that while Digby's wife was away on pilgrimage with Father Garnet to St Winifred's well in Shropshire, that Catesby revealed the plot to him. He was shocked and said he wanted to hear no more about it, but Catesby was persuasive, and it was only when he said that the Jesuits approved of the plot, that Digby was assured about it.

Everard Digby's role was to manage the Midlands and to gather as many disaffected Catholic gentry as possible to support the cause. Gathering supposedly for a hunt, they would then be appraised of the facts after the gunpowder had exploded, and they were to proceed with all haste to capture Princess Elizabeth (who would be staying nearby) and then lead a general uprising.

So a great deal was expected of him. Those who later tried to exonerate him of a major role in the plot go against the known facts.

Chapter 2

AMBROSE ROOKWOOD

Ambrose Rookwood was unlike others recruited into the plot. He was a short but handsome man, with an easy and cheerful disposition, who loved extravagant clothes. He was also one of the youngest and wealthiest of the plotters, and he was much loved in Roman Catholic circles.

He came from an old and established family, many members of which had represented Suffolk in Parliament. The family was staunchly Roman Catholic, and many of them, including Ambrose's parents, were fined and imprisoned for their beliefs. With the help of Father John Gerard, Ambrose and his two brothers and a sister were smuggled to Flanders for their education. His father died in 1600 and he inherited the estates, making Coldham Hall a common refuge for priests.

He joined the plot after being convicted of recusancy in February 1605. He wanted it to succeed to enable Catholicism to be restored to England.

FRANCIS TRESHAM

He was the first son and the oldest of eleven children of Sir Thomas Tresham and his wife, Muriel, née Throckmorton. Sir Thomas suffered extreme persecution for his adherence to the Roman Catholic faith, and, in August 1581, he was arrested and placed in the Fleet prison in London.

Tresham was Catesby's cousin and a Roman Catholic, but he seems to have little else going for him as he had a reputation for being untrustworthy and a troublemaker. A few years earlier, he had been sent to prison for a violent attack on a man (who owed his family money) and his pregnant daughter.

He was the thirteenth and last to join the group on 14 October 1605, and has been generally considered to be the traitor to the cause. His late inclusion in the plot was possibly Catesby's biggest mistake, although it may have been done in the heat of the moment with Parliament due to reassemble in just a few weeks' time. Thirteen has been considered an unlucky number because the twelve sat down at the Last Supper with Jesus, and one of them was a traitor. Unfortunately, such foolishness and superstition often accompany poor biblical understanding.

The full list of The Powder Treason Conspirators

Conspirator	Born	Place of Birth	Status in society
Thomas Bates	1570	Lapworth	Servant of the Catesbys
Robert Catesby	1573	Bushwood Hall, Lapworth?	Landowner
Sir Everard Digby	1576	Stoke Dry	Wealthy Knight of the Realm
Guido Fawkes	1570	York	Soldier
John Grant	1570?	Norbrook?	Lord of the Manor
Robert Keyes	1565	Stavely	Property Manager
Thomas Percy	1560	Scotton?	Constable of Alnwick Castle
Ambrose Rookwood	1578	Stanningfield	Wealthy Landowner
Francis Tresham	1567	Rushton	Wealthy Landowner
Robert Wintour	1565	Huddington Court	Wealthy Landowner
Thomas Wintour	1571	Huddington Court	Soldier
Christopher (Kit) Wright	1570	Plowland Hall, Welwick	Envoy
John (Jack Wright)	1568	Plowland Hall, Welwick	Gentleman of Wealth

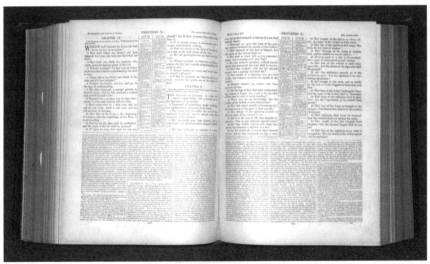

The Bible

What do you believe?

'Blessed is the man who finds wisdom, the man who gains understanding,
for she is more profitable than silver and yields better returns than
gold.' Proverbs 3:13–14

What is the place and relevance of the Bible? A misunderstanding of the Bible's position and teaching lay behind The Gunpowder Plot, and, although not all of the plotters may have been theologically knowledgeable, they did act according to their beliefs and customs.

They were inspired by clergy who were afraid to let the common people read the Scriptures for themselves; for, if they did, they would discover the supreme importance and uniqueness of the Lord Jesus Christ in regard to every area of salvation.

As a twenty-first century example, this was brought into sharp focus by the death of Pope John Paul II in April 2005. It was said by a cardinal in Rome that the Pope had 'been received into the loving arms of God and would be embraced by the Virgin Mary who would reward him for all his years faithful service to her'. Mention was made neither of Jesus and his saving work, nor of the Pope's need for repentance before death. A few days later, on Fifth Avenue in New York City, a vendor selling copies of newspapers displaying the corpse of the Pope lying in state in St Peter's, Rome, was heard to call out to those passing by, 'Look on the face of your saviour!'

This clearly goes against the plain teaching of the Bible. In John 14:6, the Bible states that Jesus is the only mediator between God and men—not Mary, Saints, Popes, Cardinals, Bishops, Priests or anyone else. He is the only way to God the Father, and none may usurp his sole position. The Protestant reformers of the sixteenth century clearly spelt this out.

Counter Reformation

Martin Luther was the powerhouse of the Protestant Reformation, but John Calvin was the one who logically and profoundly worked out the implications of the Reformation through his writings.

Galvanized by the Protestant Reformation, the Roman Catholic Church underwent a general movement of reform and missionary activity, not least through the creation of the Society of Jesus order, by Ignatius Loyola and Francis Xavier. Loyola had worked out a system for prayer, self-examination and surrender to God, which gained approval from the Pope, and then began to teach these things in the form of a catechism.

Also, to help counteract the effect of Luther, Calvin and Tyndale, another version of the Scriptures was produced. Gregory Martin translated the Bible from the Latin Vulgate into English for the benefit of English-speaking adherents of Catholicism. The New Testament was published in 1582 at Rheims, and in it is said: 'this translation was necessary because of the many false translations by Protestants which have corrupted the Word of God for they had used the Hebrew, which had been "foully corrupted by Jews, and Greeks which had been heretics".' The Old Testament was finished in 1610 at Douai, and the complete work has been known, since its revision in 1729, as the Douai/Rheims version of the Bible.

So the Protestant Reformation brought in many great changes, not least a return to the New Testament teaching regarding Christian truth. This meant that people had to make a choice regarding the true way of salvation and godly living.

Two systems of belief

WHAT THE ROMAN CATHOLIC CHURCH BELIEVES

The teaching of Roman Catholicism states that God is known today because:

- As a Prophet, Christ speaks through his church in Rome with infallibility;
- As Priest, Christ still offers himself on the altar in the Mass as really as he did on the cross, and the bread and wine at the Mass turns into the actual flesh and blood of Christ;
- As King, Christ exercises his royal authority through the hierarchy of the Roman Church.

This is at odds with what the Reformers stated to be the clear teaching of the Bible. For tradition, however good, only muddies the waters. God's Word alone must be the final authority for Christian truth.

PROTESTANTS BELIEVE
Protestant teaching states that God is revealed through:
- Christ on Calvary as the one and only and all-sufficient sacrifice for sin;
- Jesus Christ is the only High Priest through whom sinners can come to God;
- The Throne of Grace the only confessional, because the blood of Jesus Christ gives access to God the Heavenly Father through the work of God the Holy Spirit.

When compared, the differences become readily apparent, and, to make them easy to memorize, the Reformers coined several terms (each one commencing 'Sola', or 'only'), so that ordinary people could grasp the wonderful truth of God that alone is revealed in the Bible.

Reformation Principles
Martin Luther's stand encouraged many others to question the practices of their time, and five things became the rallying call for their position. They were:

1. *SOLA SCRIPTURA*—THE SCRIPTURE ALONE
The Bible is seen as the full and final authority that God has given to people regarding everything to do with life, so it is the only authority for life and faith, and God's voice is most clearly heard when the Bible is read or preached. But how should a person respond to the Bible and its teaching?

2. *SOLA FIDE*—FAITH ALONE
Faith is believing in God and his Word. It is his gracious gift to sinners to enable them to put their trust in him. It means that a person can do nothing to save himself or herself, but it is the free gift of God. But in what (or, in whom) is the sinner to place his or her trust?

3. *SOLUS CHRISTUS*—IN CHRIST ALONE
The Bible clearly teaches in 1 Timothy 2:5 that 'there is one God and one

mediator between God and men, the man Christ Jesus'. However, people have to understand that they cannot approach God by their own efforts, and something else has to be understood.

4. *SOLA GRATIA*—BY GRACE ALONE
No one is able to save himself or to build up enough merit points for God to say: 'What a good person this is; I will save him, and let him into heaven.' Salvation is all of God's mercy and his wonderful grace. So, pilgrimages, offerings and lifestyle are not able to save—God alone is able to do that, and he pours out his love as he sees fit. God cannot be packaged to suit human beings, neither can he be told what to do and when to do it, for, to be truly God, he must be free from human constraint. That is another truth that the Reformers showed to the world. Salvation is not primarily for the sake of any individual, but to show how great God is in every area of life.

5. *SOLI DEO GLORIA*—FOR GOD'S GLORY ALONE
So often people enjoy basking in reflected glory, to be in the slipstream of others so that they might be considered as celebrities. The Reformation sought to redress this and to reassert that God and his glory alone were all that mattered.

The effects of the Reformation were far reaching, so that even music came to represent the battles that had taken place. Felix Mendelssohn (1809–1847) called his fifth symphony *The Reformation*. The choice of subject was indicative of Mendelssohn's devout Lutheran faith. It includes a chorale fantasy on Luther's mighty hymn, 'A Safe Stronghold our God is still' and it is performed all over the world today, standing as a musical testimony to the tremendous effects of the events in sixteenth-century Europe.

A matter of life and death
Crucial questions concerning the Bible and its place in common life had brought conflict into England. The battle lines had been drawn firmly at Little Sudbury Manor in Gloucestershire by William Tyndale.

A learned man had been debating some point over the table, and finding he could not get the better of this troublesome scripture-quoting priest he rose in a rage and stormed,

'We were better be without God's law than the pope's.' That, thought Tyndale, aptly summarized the prevailing view in the Church of Rome. He broke the pregnant silence that followed: 'I defy the pope and all his laws; if God spare my life, ere many years I will cause a boy that driveth a plough shall know more of the scripture than thou doest.'[1]

So it was that he set about his life's work, the placing of a copy of the Bible in English in the hands of the common people. This action would eventually lead to the fire and a stake outside Vilvorde Castle, Belgium, on 6 October 1536, where he would be put to death.

Wonder-working hands

Tyndale's stand and translation caused trouble because the priests and prelates could no longer hide behind the Latin text of the Scriptures, when choosing to disclose that what they said on a given subject was the plain teaching of the Bible. 'The priest then was the indispensable man, and there was no getting to heaven but through his hands. Only the priest's hands could touch the bread and the wine and consecrate them, changing them through the sacrament into the flesh and blood of Christ. Only the priest's hands could make the sign of the cross giving absolution from sins. These were the hands that gave meaning to "good works", whether that meant buying wax or founding a college. They made the difference between salvation and perdition.'[3]

War and violence

Another problem that is often ignored was the use or misuse of the warrior and violence passages of the Bible. How should they be interpreted, and what relevance do they have for daily life? This was a vital question, yet many chose to limit their interpretation to achieve the ends which they desired.

There is no denying the fact that some of the Bible passages, particularly the narrative ones that deal with violent things, can be difficult to interpret. But surely this means that great care must be taken before basing a course of action in the present on a Bible event of the past, particularly if the context and meaning is not fully understood. Regarding the Old Testament details of wholesale or individual slaughter that cause many people to consider the God of the Old Testament to be different from the God of the New

Testament, we should remember that nowhere are we told to emulate the practices of the Children of Israel, or the Judges, or Kings. It is never safe to assume that God expects his people in the present to act in the same way as people did in the times of the Scriptures, unless, of course, there is a specific command and that it is crystal clear for them to do so.

Since the time of the New Testament, 2 Corinthians 10:3–4 has been the controlling text: 'For though we live in the world, we do not wage war as the world does. The weapons we fight with are not the weapons of the world. On the contrary, they have divine power to demolish strongholds.' The Christian is to use the weapons that God has supplied for this spiritual warfare and they are clearly listed in Ephesians 6:10–18. Yet some people may argue that the very words of Jesus go against this, for in Matthew 10:34 he said, 'Do not suppose that I have come to bring peace on the earth. I did not come to bring peace, but a sword.' The key to understanding this statement is twofold, firstly the context and, secondly, what he meant by the word 'sword'. The context is that of the sending out the twelve disciples to 'the lost sheep of Israel' (10:6), that is, to the Jewish people. Secondly, in referring to a sword, they would have thought of the *gladius*, the favoured weapon of the Roman army. It was the sword that conquered. It was about two feet six inches long (75 cm) by two inches (5 cm) wide and was a sharp, double-edged sword. The Bible refers to God's Word in Hebrews 4:12–13 as 'the word of God [which] is living and active. Sharper than any double-edged sword, it penetrates even to dividing soul and spirit, joints and marrow; it judges the thoughts and attitudes of the heart. Nothing in all creation is hidden from God's sight. Everything is uncovered and laid bare before the eyes of him to whom we must give account.'

So Jesus was going to divide and conqueror through the use of God's Word. This was, of course, the great Reformation principle, that when God's Word was preached, God's voice was heard, and God's work was begun in the lives of people. In Matthew 10, this is what is recorded: 'As you go, preach this message' (verse 7), and then, 'But when they arrest you, do not worry about what to say or how to say it. At that time you will be given what to say, for it will not be you speaking, but the Spirit of your Father speaking through you' (verses 19 and 20). Ephesians 6:17 states that 'the sword of the Spirit ... is the word of God.'

This sword is meant to be used not just for attack but also for defence, and, in Genesis 3:24, God placed 'cherubim and a flaming sword flashing back and forth to guard the way to the tree of life'. The sword was God's living word, and Adam and Eve could not go beyond what he had decreed, and so they were banished from Eden into the wider world by God's word, and because of God's word they could not return to Paradise.

When Robert Catesby either decided to become a terrorist or was set up to deal with those in power in such a final and brutal fashion, it was claimed that God's blessing was on the venture. That only happened because the Bible had been misunderstood or manipulated. The familiar wicked ideology was set in place and the drama started to unfold, and we all do well to notice this lesson from history.

Does it really matter?

These are relevant things, for there are some who claim to be given words directly from God. It is not uncommon, during an open time in some Christian services of worship, to hear people claim that they have a direct word from God for the congregation. The medieval priest could have claimed the same thing and told people that to disobey what he said was to go against God. Now that is the danger, for the speaker can rightly claim that if he or she has a direct word from God, then it should be given an equal or higher place than that of the Bible, and to ignore or to disobey that person's word would be sinful.

Reformation teaching disagrees profoundly with that viewpoint, and emphasizes that the Bible alone is the full and final word on any subject relating to doctrine and faith.

Fidei Defensor on a current coin of the realm

The legacy of history

'Trust in the LORD with all your heart and lean not on your own understanding; in all your ways acknowledge him, and he will make your paths straight.' Proverbs 3:5–6

England, Spain, Rome and the Church across Europe were the four big players involved in the drama that was played out in Westminster in the autumn of 1605, and to understand the enormity of what was planned, a brief overview of the history of the times will bring clarity to the unfolding drama.

In England in the sixteenth and seventeenth centuries, as in other places across Europe, the state church appeared to be in disarray, as more Bible translations in local languages appeared in many countries. These had the effect of exposing errors of teaching by the clergy.

Various monarchs and lesser rulers, as well as the papacy, had a vested interest in what was unfolding in such a dramatic way in Stuart England, and it all came about because of a long chain of significant events.

A shot in the eye

In the autumn of 1066, two battles were fought that changed not only English history but also the landscape of England. The first took place on 25 September at Stamford Bridge, eight miles to the east of York, where King Harold, after an astonishing forced march from London, arrived with his troops not only to surprise the Viking army, but also to defeat them soundly. Such was the scale of his victory, that sixty years later the pile of bones that his victorious army had left on the battlefield was still a local landmark.

Harold, however, could not rest on his laurels, for he then heard that the Normans had taken advantage of his being in the north and had landed at Pevensey in Sussex in the south of his kingdom. Now the same incredible journey had to be undertaken by Harold's troops, but this time in the other direction. He arrived to find William of Normandy—who felt irked that Harold had gone back on an agreement that he, William, should become king after the death of Edward the Confessor—dug in near Hastings, and, on 14 October, one of the most famous battles in history took place. Harold held all the cards but he was defeated, and, as the Bayeux Tapestry famously depicts, he was wounded by an arrow in the right eye, before being cut to pieces by mounted knights.

Now the landscape would be changed dramatically: 'After the conquest of 1066 the comfortable Old Saxon Minsters were torn down and replaced by huge Romanesque Cathedrals which still stand as memorials to the Norman victory.'[1] So across the countryside, totally dwarfing the humble dwellings of many people, mighty cathedrals and minsters soared into the air, primarily to proclaim that the Normans were there and that they were there to stay. They were an overwhelming symbol of occupation, and, until relatively recently, were the largest and tallest structures to be seen in many cities across England. The Norman kings, therefore, left a legacy that others were able to exploit.

Compared with Britain and the Continent today, the kings and queens of European history often wielded supreme power, even though in many cases their powers were ill-defined. The monarch often had no standing army, was frequently short of finance, and had to govern bearing in mind the need to maintain the good will of the people, especially of the land-owning gentry who were so often the natural leaders in society, but who were also, at times, more powerful than the king himself. English history has many examples of this such as Magna Carta, involving King John and the Barons. Such examples also include Sir Roger de Mortimer in 1227–1230, Simon De Montfort in 1265 and Henry Percy in 1405 (also known as Harry Hotspur—after whom Tottenham Hotspur, the famous football team, is named!), as well as during the time of the Wars of the Roses between 1462 and 1485.

Enter the King

King Henry VIII was a colossus who bestrode the nation and influenced it greatly in the sixteenth century. As a young man, he was handsome, intelligent, and, for many, the perfect embodiment of royalty. If kings were to have a model, it was Henry in his prime, but, as he matured, he became less tolerant and more of a tyrant. A big man with a big personality, he was a formidable opponent; therefore many tried to keep in favour with him, regardless of the cost.

In 1521, the Pope had given Henry VIII the title 'Defender of the Faith'; this was in response to a paper that Henry had written, with the help of Sir Thomas More, called, *The Defence of the Seven Sacraments* against, as he considered him, 'that Protestant heretic, Martin Luther'.

Luther was a German monk who had been very worried about his eternal welfare. However, he came to understand the gospel, and God graciously saved him, so Luther then turned his attention to the state of the Church. He saw that it needed reforming and that many of its members were held in bondage by its unbiblical teaching and abuses. Also, he was against the materialism of the Roman Church, and he attacked its methods of accumulating wealth through such fraudulent means (principally by selling indulgences, pledges, with the implication that in buying these things, the purchaser was helped to get out of purgatory and into heaven). Luther had stated most forcibly that the Pope had no authority to forgive sins, and he maintained that it was faith in Christ alone that could do that. He also said that people did not need priests to mediate with God on their behalf, for, if they were true believers, they could hear God speaking to them through his Word, the Bible, and they could talk to him through prayer.

The result of things such as this may still be seen on the British coins of the realm with the initials FD (*Fidei Defensor*). The present monarch, Queen Elizabeth II, is still considered to be Defender of the Faith, but one may well wonder whether this will continue to be the case in successive generations of royalty.

The King's great matter

Henry VIII had married Catherine of Aragon, the wife of his deceased brother, Alfred, because he said: 'I am obeying my father's dying wish.' Catherine was married to Henry for nearly twenty years; she bore several sons but they had all died. One daughter, Mary, was born in 1516, and no one expected Catherine to have any more children. Despite this, she was greatly respected. However, Henry desperately wanted a son, and he was determined to do all he could to achieve that end to ensure his line would continue. So his 'great matter' dominated all, and he sought a divorce from Catherine, but she had only one answer: 'I am your own true wife.' It greatly helped her that her nephew, the Emperor Charles V, the most powerful ruler in Europe, had just taken the Pope prisoner, and only the Pope could grant Henry a divorce. So, in seeking a way out of this dilemma, Henry decided to turn to the Bible to see what arguments he could muster for his stance and requirements.

What shall I try to make the Bible say?

As a scholar who prided himself as a theologian, it may appear a little surprising that Henry could be so selective in the way he used the Bible, but he wanted solutions, and the finer details of biblical interpretation only got in his way. To legitimize his divorce from Catherine of Aragon, he turned to Leviticus 20:21, which stated that a man should not take his brother's wife, for they would be childless. Henry had been punished, so the argument ran, because he had transgressed God's law, and so he would not have a living son by Catherine. However, Catherine stated firmly that as her first husband, Arthur, was so young, just fifteen when he had died, they had never consummated their marriage, and she had been a virgin when she married Henry.

In fact, the text of Leviticus 20:21 refers to childlessness, and says nothing about 'sons' as Henry had misinterpreted it; had not Catherine produced Mary? Even more to the point were the words of Deuteronomy 25:5, where a man is actually encouraged to marry his deceased brother's wife in order to carry on the family line. There is no contradiction between these two verses, for Leviticus speaks of a living brother, whereas Deuteronomy makes provision for the widow after the brother has died. Henry would have known this, yet he chose to be blinded to this teaching and to distort it for his use.

Henry would also have known the account of King David and Bathsheba, the wife of Uriah the Hittite, as recorded in 2 Samuel 11–12. David lusted after this man's wife, and arranged for him to be killed. After the deed had been accomplished, David was visited by the prophet Nathan who not only pronounced judgement on David, but also told him that his young son would die. The lesson of history was there to be seen if only

Henry would read and think about it. Henry needed to see that judgement always follows on from sinful acts.

The trouble with sex

Another text that should have caused this scholarly king to take stock of what he was doing is found in 1 Corinthians 6:16, where the apostle Paul writes to the Christian church: 'Do you not know that he who unites himself with a prostitute is one with her in body? For it is said, "The two will become one flesh."' Licentious living is condemned in the Bible, and it does not take a great intellect to work out the wider implications stated in that text. If two people come together sexually, they are considered to be one flesh, whether or not one of them is a prostitute, and this, in the sight of God, is almost as though they were married! This has staggering implications not just for Henry VIII, but also for all people who indulge in casual sexual relations. Indeed, there is no such thing as casual sex because there is no such thing as a casual God.

Henry, with his reputation as bluff King Hal, the man about town, one of 'the lads', should have taken care, for God judges the foolish actions of all, whether king or commoner, both in this life as well as in the life to come. But Henry never did take care; instead of showing contrition and repentance, he was always blaming someone else, and it would be that person's fault if he did not have what he desired. As a result, some of the brightest luminaries of his court would ultimately pay the price for his disappointment, the most famous ones being Sir Thomas More and Thomas Cromwell.

In his permissive will, God overruled the foolishness of Henry, and allowed the events that caused such a dramatic transformation to the life and practice of the population of England to take place. As a result, Henry discovered that he was not in control as he thought he was going to be.

A new head

The year 1534 is another key date in English history, for, in that year, King Henry VIII finally severed ties with Rome and made himself head of the Church in England. The King's advisors, led by Thomas Cromwell, created the theory of Royal Supremacy, and Henry VIII used this new power to sanction the dissolution of the monasteries and nunneries, thus gaining a great deal of wealth through his actions.

These things enraged Rome in general and the Pope in particular, so, in 1535, the Pope made Archbishop Fisher a cardinal. In retaliation, Henry swore to send 'Fisher's head to Rome to fit his new hat'. Fisher was beheaded, but his head was placed on a spike alongside Sir Thomas More's on old London Bridge in 1535.

Rome's desperation for revenge at this outrage made it like an evil spider at the centre of its web, putting out probes to see who could be caught. The Papacy needed someone to bring England back into the fold and clean up this situation. Spain, considered to be more Catholic than Rome itself, answered the call. Two powerful monarchs, Ferdinand (1452–1516), and Isabella (1451–1502), had been personally involved in England's history. Their beloved daughter was Catherine of Aragon who had been briefly married to Prince Arthur but, on his death, had become the bride of Henry VIII. Now that he had unfairly divorced her in favour of Anne Boleyn, Spain was enraged, and conflict was inevitable. This was ultimately to set the scene for events up to and including The Gunpowder Plot.

In November 1478, Ferdinand and Isabella had set up the inquisition in Spain under the leadership of Isabella's confessor, a fanatical monk called Tomas de Torquemada. Although those monarchs were by then dead, Spain was still prepared to come to the aid of one of their own who had been slighted, cast off, and very unfairly proclaimed illegitimate by England's Parliament.

The situation was further exacerbated because two of the women that Henry had married had produced daughters, Queen Catherine's (Aragon) was Mary Tudor who would become Mary I and is also known as Bloody Mary. Queen Anne's (Boleyn) was Elizabeth I, the Virgin Queen who would epitomize glory and power as her empire expanded across the world. Before Mary and Elizabeth could occupy the throne they had to wait while another, their half-brother Edward, son of Queen Jane (Seymour), took up the reigns of leadership.

A boy with a man's head on his shoulders

Edward became king when his father, Henry VIII, died on 28 January 1547, exactly one hundred years after his grandfather, Henry VII, had been born (28 January 1447). Edward, being only nine years of age, was provided with advisors, and Edward Seymour became the Lord Protector. This young monarch was privileged to live at a time when God had kindly given England men of the calibre of Hugh Latimer and Nicolas Ridley, whose rich and powerful ministries blessed the lives of many, not least the young man now on the throne.

As he grew and matured, Edward showed increasing adherence to the Protestant faith, and was supportive of the sweeping changes taking place in the country carried out by Archbishop Thomas Cranmer and his fellow reformers. The most striking was the introduction of Thomas Cranmer's magnificent *Book of Common Prayer* that was placed before Parliament in 1548, and, being part of the 'Act of Uniformity', came into force in June 1549. One thing that did disturb Edward was the continuing and stubborn adherence to the old faith on the part of his half-sister Mary, yet he was not to live long enough to be able to persuade her to change her views. There was a real and perceived threat from Roman Catholicism to the new English way of life, and Edward wanted to stifle all the threats to the new faith that was now transforming his kingdom.

The spread of Protestant teaching or Calvinism (as it became known) was pervasive and persuasive. To some, it was paradoxical that Calvinism had its origins in the land of England's old enemy, France, and that they were now being conquered by a Frenchman, John Calvin, who used words rather than guns.

Trouble looms

In 1553, Edward VI, at the age of sixteen, died of tuberculosis aggravated by an attack of measles. John Knox, the great Scottish Reformer, said, 'We had a king of so godly disposition towards virtue and the truth of God, that none from the beginning passed him, and to my knowledge, none of his years did ever match him.'

So it was on 19 July, that Edward's half-sister Mary, daughter of Catherine of Aragon and granddaughter of Ferdinand and Isabella, succeeded to the throne as Queen Mary I. This took place only after a power struggle in which Lady Jane Grey was to die as a pawn of state, a crime which many rank as fearful and as foul as any committed during the reign of Henry VIII.

Now the new Protestant adherents would soon discover that the eldest daughter of Henry VIII could be just as cruel and unfeeling as her father.

Timescale of King Henry VIII's break with Rome

1529		Henry VIII summons the Reformation Parliament.
1529	18 June	Catherine of Aragon begins to contest Henry's application for a divorce.
1532		'Submission of the clergy', a law that prevented the clergy from independently passing laws without the knowledge and consent of the laity in Parliament.
1532		Act diverting 'First fruits and Annates (Clerical taxes)' from Rome to the English crown.
1532		'Dispensations Act'—This stopped all payments to Rome.
1533	25 January	Henry secretly marries Anne Boleyn.
1533		'Act in Restraint of Appeals to Rome'—This deprived the papacy of any right to judge English cases in either Church or State.
1533	23 May	Henry officially divorces Catherine of Aragon.
1533	22 June	Bishop John Fisher executed.
1533	6 July	Thomas More executed.
1534		'Act of Supremacy'—Henry was declared the head of the Church in England.
1536		'Act of Dissolution of the smaller Monasteries'.
1536	19 May	Anne Boleyn executed on Tower Green in the Tower of London.
1536	6 October	The martyrdom of William Tyndale in Belgium.
1537		Henry sanctions a London printing of Miles Coverdale's Bible.
1538	5 September	Henry VIII orders every Church in England to display one book of the whole Bible of the largest volume in English.
1539		'Act of Dissolution of the greater Monasteries'.
1539		The Great Bible appears and is officially sanctioned.
1540		The last of the monasteries surrendered and the process was complete.

English Monarchs

King Henry VIII

King Edward VI

Queen Mary I

Queen Elizabeth I

King James I

The fiery queen

'Do not be wise in your own eyes; fear the LORD and shun evil. This will bring health to your body and nourishment to your bones,' Proverbs 3:7–8

The seeds of The Gunpowder plot were planted in the reign of King Henry VIII, and, during his daughter's reign, its shoots began to sprout, for Mary was advised that the way to cleanse the land of heresy was through fire. It takes only a short journey in the imagination to see how, fifty-two years later, gunpowder could be intended to produce a conflagration that would clean up Royalty, Parliament, Religion and the Nation in one go.

Mary Tudor was probably the most unhappy and unsuccessful of English monarchs. Having been brought up at her father's court with all ceremony due to the heiress to the throne, including her being betrothed at different times to European heirs, she became a young and traumatized victim of her father's lust. When her mother, Catherine of Aragon, fell out of favour and Anne Boleyn replaced her at the King's side, Mary was declared illegitimate by an act of Parliament and she was excluded from the privileges she had enjoyed until that time. Her half-sister, Elizabeth, and then her half-brother, Edward, overshadowed her at court. She was told to give up her Roman Catholic religion and embrace the new faith, but the Spanish blood flowed strongly in her veins, and she stubbornly refused to change, clinging on to her confessors and chapel. It was not unknown for her to attend the Roman Catholic Mass six times a day.

I need a man

Mary was proclaimed Queen on 19 July 1553. Parliament annulled the divorce of Catherine of Aragon, established Mary's legitimacy, and promised to restore the Church to its former position.

Soon after she ascended to the throne, Mary dispatched a messenger to Rome, with the following missive: 'I am your faithful daughter and England has returned to the Roman obedience.' To reinforce this action, she released the Roman Catholics Gardiner and Bonner from the Tower of London, and they were given prestigious appointments: Gardiner became Bishop of Winchester with a fine palace on the south bank of the River Thames at Southwark, and Bonner became Bishop of London. Eventually, they were to make up a triumvirate of power with Reginald Pole, the Pope's Cardinal and Legate.

Try though they would, one thing Mary and her advisors could not do was to restore to the Church the lands that her father, Henry VIII, had seized when he dissolved the monasteries in 1536. Although many of the most powerful landowners might be happy to attend the Mass without any qualm of conscience, they were not prepared to hand back what they now thought of as being rightfully theirs, and therefore Mary's reforms would never be fully implemented.

Even though she was thirty-seven years old when she became Queen, a male heir was desirable. However, there was a sticking point, for her husband would be very powerful, and therein lay the problem. If the Queen were to marry an English nobleman, other powerful aristocrats would be jealous, as his family would be elevated to the determent of others, and civil war might ensue. But if she married a foreign ruler, England may be tied to an alien country, whose ways and laws might be imposed on the English, and as a proud island race the people did not want outside interference.

Let's go to Spain

Mary, who was always more Spanish than English and never truly understood the people she reigned over, decided to look to her mother country for a suitor. The Emperor (both Charles V of Austria, and Charles I of Spain at one and the same time) was at one point considered to be a suitable match, but he decided not to marry again. His sympathies were with the people of the Netherlands (but whether they appreciated it is open to question). Instead, Charles entrusted his ambassador, Simon Renard (who went on to become one of Mary's closest advisors), with the express purpose of presenting to Mary, his son, Phillip II, as a suitable husband. Later on, Renard caused considerable difficulty, and Mary had to circumvent the irritation of her councillors when they complained about him, for she allowed him to enter her royal apartments in disguise via a back entrance.

The differences between the couple were considerable, for Mary was by now thirty-eight, and Philip twenty-six years of age. Mary was small in stature, and because she had gained weight, looked squat. Also she appeared prematurely worn, and having an indifferent complexion with thinning hair, and an almost mannish voice. This, coupled with a great appetite for religion, did not appear to make her suitable for any king. By contrast, Philip was small, slender, had blue eyes, was blond, bearded with a fair complexion and was lascivious. He was not a consort who would see beyond the outward appearance of a woman, and nor would he seek a long-term relationship with a woman after losing interest in her.

After some delay, because her English subjects were not enthralled by the proposed union, a marriage treaty was drawn up that seemed propitious to Mary and to the country at large. The treaty included the following stipulations.

- Philip should respect the laws and not interfere with the rights and liberties of Englishmen.
- The power of conferring titles and offices should remain with the Queen.
- Foreigners to the English were not to be given office.
- Any issue of the marriage, should it be male, was to be heir to the English crown, and to Spanish possessions in the Low Countries and Burgundy.
- The Queen would not be forced to leave England unless she desired to do so.
- If Mary should die, Philip was to claim no right to the throne.

This treaty was very favourable from the English point of view, but Spanish interference in the affairs of state caused a general outcry when its contents were published, because Spain, above all nations, had acquired a contemporary reputation for cruelty. Mary, therefore, was in great danger, especially when Sir Thomas Wyatt, in response, moved in rebellion on the capital. If he had pressed home his advantage, she would have undoubtedly been captured and probably killed. But his lack of decisive action cost him and a number of others dearly, and they paid the ultimate price for being traitors to the crown.

Fire on the horizon

Her chosen consort, Philip II of Spain, was the most ardent supporter of the Inquisition, and a perceivable shift in its mission was seen, as it veered away from purifying the faith to protecting papal power under his leadership.

Philip was preparing to leave Spain for England as Wyatt's rebellion was subdued, and he was determined to bring England fully back into the Church of Rome, and to achieve this, he appointed Bartolome de Carranza y Miranda as Archbishop of Toledo and, eventually, as the Primate of all Spain.

Carranza was an intellectual and was soon deeply resented by the English, who nicknamed him the black friar because of his Dominican robes. Being accustomed to the methods employed in Spain to deal with heretics, he has gone down in history as the architect of one England's darkest periods, namely the Marian persecutions, which culminated in the fires at Smithfield and elsewhere. He was so hated that a number of attempts were made on his life—but he survived them all.

Mary married Philip at Winchester Cathedral on 25 July 1554, with Bishop Gardiner performing the ceremony. A few weeks later, the couple entered London, in a brilliant display, but there were signs of unrest. The English distrusted the Spanish and their motives, and there were outbreaks of violence between the two nationalities. These culminated in a number of hangings.

Increasing efforts were now made to turn England fully back to Rome and, to facilitate this, Cardinal Pole was dispatched to give the English absolution from their sin of heresy and to reconcile them with the Church of Rome. This was achieved on 28 November 1554 when he stood in front of Parliament.

Both the marriage and Mary's subsequent supposed pregnancy immensely strengthened her hand, for Parliament, in grateful response, restored Roman Catholicism. But the euphoria did not last, and things started to unravel when the pregnancy proved to be false. Philip, who was growing increasingly bored with his older wife, started to turn his hungry eyes upon Elizabeth, Mary's younger half-sister.

However, in September 1555, Philip, tiring of both Mary and Elizabeth, left to join his father in Flanders. He had felt slighted because Parliament refused to have him crowned King of England. He left Carranza behind to be Mary's advisor and to shake up the troublesome English. As a result of the desertion of her husband, Mary became increasingly morose and convinced that the failure of her marriage was due to divine vengeance. Like her father before her, she used the Bible in a selective fashion, for in her thinking she was being punished for the Protestant heresies still practised in England, and so the burning of heretics became more frequent.

Parliament had passed the act for the punishment of heretics, the statute 'de heretico comburendo' in 1555, because Mary and her advisors thought that religious peace was impossible without these fanatics being silenced.

Death by fire was considered to be the most appropriate method of punishment, for it not only cleansed but also removed that which was ugly, tainted and unwanted—and it also saved on space, as a burial plot would not be needed!

Brutal treatment

Under Henry VIII and Edward VI, people had been burned alive, and prominent clergymen like Thomas Cranmer, Nicholas Ridley and Hugh Latimer had played their part in those events, even to the point of preaching the sermon before the fires were lit. But extreme cruelty breeds barbarism, and the events that transpired between the years 1555 and 1558, were, for England, times of unprecedented barbarism. In under four years, 227 men and 56 women were burned at the stake, twice as many as in the previous 150 years. Mary achieved a faster rate of executions through religious persecution than the contemporary Spanish Inquisition, which is why the Protestant martyrs are remembered. Some, like Cranmer, Ridley and Latimer, were people in high profile, but the majority of victims were from the lower classes, and there were some particularly nasty death scenes. It would appear, however, that the death of Thomas Cranmer, who played such a prominent role under Henry VIII in the divorce of Catherine of Aragon and the marriage of Anne Boleyn, might have had more to do with revenge then heresy.

Mary, stubborn and strong-willed by nature, failed to regard compromise as anything but a betrayal of weakness. She and her advisors seemed honestly to believe that they were applying the only remedy suitable for the removal of a great disease from the church, and, as they considered that heresy was at an unprecedented high, what they did was on an unprecedented scale. The plotters of 1605 would have fully endorsed this viewpoint, and it may be that they would have used this kind of reasoning as justification for their actions many years later.

Mary's dowry

In medieval England, the land had been referred to as the Virgin Mary's dowry. Thomas Arundel, Archbishop of Canterbury, wrote in 1400, 'We English being the servants of her special inheritance, and her Dowry, as we are commonly called, ought to surpass others in the fervour of our praise and devotion.'

During Mary's reign, the Bible was again misunderstood and wrongly used to reinforce this, because Mary believed she most closely represented the Virgin Mary in the Bible. She suffered from spiritual pride and when her priests and propagandists told her that she was the second Mary, Virgin and Queen; she believed them with a simple, devastating literalness.

Like her namesake, she was humbled yet exalted and even before her false pregnancy she swelled with a God-given certainty. God had chosen her to be his instrument to restore England to the faith; God had chosen Philip, like a latter-day Joseph, to be her spouse; God had made her pregnant, let no man think otherwise. Armed with these invincible certainties, this otherwise modest and merciful woman found the strength to brush aside her parliament, bully her council, and burn and brutalize dissenters.[1]

The principal reason why Roman Catholicism was never successfully re-established during Mary's reign was because she only ruled for five years. After two phantom pregnancies, on 17 November 1558, Mary died in great pain of ovarian or cervical cancer, which was the probable cause of her abdominal swelling—not pregnancy as she had believed it to be. It is said that her last words were not about her unpopularity but over the loss of Calais, which came about because Philip II had involved England in Spain's war with France. Her heart and bowels were buried in the Chapel Royal at St James Palace, and her corpse was buried in Westminster Abbey, which seems to symbolize her divided interests between her native Spain and the English she sought to control.

Mary was placed in her tomb in Westminster Abbey, which was paid for by her half-sister Elizabeth. It seems ironic that Elizabeth's last resting place would be above Mary's, and that her heavy tomb is now pressing down on Mary's so that some restoration work will probably be required in the near future. But, considering her place in history, it may seem symbolically right that Mary, who would be completely overshadowed by Elizabeth, is permanently under her!

Gloriana

Mary's passing, along with the accession of Elizabeth to the Tudor throne, was greeted with relief by many people. When Elizabeth heard that she was to be Queen on 17 November 1558, she was at Hatfield House in Hertfordshire. The nobleman who broke the news to her, found that Elizabeth was in the grounds sitting under a tree reading her Greek New Testament. Overcome with emotion, and probably relief that she was not going to be sent to the Tower of London to die like her mother, she eventually kneeled on the grass and quoted part of Psalm 118, 'This is the Lord's doing and it is marvellous in our eyes.'

So the insufferable Protestant, Elizabeth I, came to the throne, but she was not going to be left in peace. In 1570, the Pope, fed up with her and her policies, decreed that English Roman Catholics did not have to obey her, and to emphasize the point, he excommunicated Elizabeth. This meant that English Catholics were being actively encouraged by a foreign power to become traitors to the crown, and this fuelled Protestant fear of Catholics. Spain, then a European superpower (and, of all European nations, it was rightly to be feared), was financing many plots to get rid of Elizabeth. In 1588, it sent its almost invincible Armada against Elizabeth. It was organized by Philip II, Mary's former husband, who, turning his sights on England, sent an immense invasion force, a vast armada of 130 ships against the English. It did not succeed, the weather being the principal reason. Philip's fleet was destroyed, although Sir Francis Drake has become credited with the victory.

Hampton Court Palace

A new Bible

'She is a tree of life to those who embrace her; those who lay hold of her will be blessed.' Proverbs 3:18

In 1566 another Mary, the Queen of Scots, had given birth to a boy named James, who succeeded to the throne of Scotland a few months later as James VI. This little boy was to be involved in the history of England in a way that would probably have amazed those who attended his birth in Scotland, for, at that time, Elizabeth was still firmly on the English throne and she was not going to relinquish her power. But when death finally took her, James was ready to step in. In Scotland, James had waited to come and fulfil his great mission in life, but now he would need help to succeed in ruling a people that he did not know. For their part, the English had little understanding of what they were getting in the person of their new king.

The king's champion

Help was not far away, for, hovering in the background and never far from the action was Robert Cecil, a man who made himself indispensable in the affairs of state. His father, William Cecil, First Lord Burghley, had shown remarkable staying power and skill in outliving both Queens, Roman Catholic and Protestant.

Robert Cecil, First Earl of Salisbury, followed in his father's footsteps by becoming Elizabeth's Secretary of State in 1596, and his years of control smoothed the passage for James to ascend the English throne. He negotiated the peace terms that ended the long war with Spain in 1604, and, as a consequence, dealt a severe blow to the plans of the plotters, although they still seemed to think that Spain would welcome the chance of invading England. James came to rely on Robert Cecil's advice and more then once benefited from the network of spies that Cecil controlled throughout the land. No doubt, he inherited some of these spies from Elizabeth's cousin and spy master, Sir Francis Walsingham. He served James well and often had to work by himself as the King preferred to be out hunting rather then attending to matters of state.

But just what was his Lord and master really like?

James the King of England

James was a small, awkward, loudmouthed, pedantic, ungainly and uncouth man, who was described as 'the wisest fool in Christendom' because his succession brought the union of the English and Scottish crowns that had been longed for over many turbulent years. Amazingly, many people in England were surprised when they first met him to discover that James spoke with a strong Scots accent—hardly surprising for a Scotsman!

He enjoyed accepting praise and applause for his wit and looks; this was ironic, as he was not known for clean habits, washing only occasionally and having a somewhat dishevelled appearance. Because he rarely washed his hands, James had a preference for wearing gloves, and, for the few who saw or touched his naked hands, the experience was unforgettable—it was like touching old black leather!

James was also unfortunate in that his tongue was rather large for his mouth, and he was inclined to slobber when eating food or kissing his handsome young men. His court was tainted by financial and sexual scandals. James was a practising homosexual and had great contempt for women, though he managed to father six children!

Roman Catholics were encouraged by the early signs of his reign, for he displayed a relaxed attitude towards them, and they thought he would restore the supremacy of Rome, especially as he was the son of Mary Queen of Scots. Strangely and illogically, some Roman Catholics believed in the 'mother's merits', that is, those spiritual benefits gained by Mary Queen of Scots' martyrdom—as they consider it to be—which would mean that God would look in kindness upon them, and, by his grace, James would be converted to Catholicism. His wife, Anne of Denmark, had converted to Catholicism and therefore it seemed to be only a matter of time before James did so, too.

Disappointingly, though, he did not act as they had hoped for, and whatever promises, verbal or written, that he had made to them while he was in Scotland, have not survived intact. Suffice it to say that many felt let down, and, as a consequence, a number of Catholic conspiracies were hatched against him.

Hampton Court Palace

What really launched the Gunpowder Plot seems to have come about as a result of a proclamation James had issued on 24 October 1603 for a two-day conference of senior clergy that would convene at Hampton Court Palace in January 1604.

At the conference, James tried unsuccessfully to accommodate as many divergent views as possible, and, in trying to please all, he ended up pleasing none. He had embraced the middle ground, and, as a Scot, he had unwittingly followed a very English trait. Describing this position, a former Bishop of London wrote:

The Church of England is unlike most other Churches in that it claims to be both ancient and modern. Its services are those of the Great Church descending from apostolic times, moulded by the Fathers, developed by medieval churchmen, translated into the English tongue, and remodelled at the Reformation. Because it has links with the past it can hold out its hand in friendship to Churches of the Catholic tradition. At the same time, because it was strongly influenced by the Reformation it can live on friendly terms with Churches of the Evangelical type.[1]

James could not have stated his position in any clearer terms.

An unloved Bible version

The King and his bishops had never liked the Geneva Bible, especially the notes in the margin, so, when it was suggested by John Reynolds that a new authoritative version of the Bible be published, it appeared that James had been given a gift that would answer any critic who said the Hampton Court conference had not produced anything worth while. Also, as the Douai/Rheims Bible was being worked on, there was a very real danger that many copies of it would enter England to the detriment of the Protestant cause. So approval was given for a new Bible, and the King James (Authorized) Version is the only significant achievement readily accredited to James; it is still read widely in the twenty-first century.

Within a few weeks of the conclusion of the Hampton Court conference, increasingly harsher penalties were imposed, and in February 1604, James publicly announced his 'utter detestation' of Catholicism. Within days, many priests and Jesuits were rounded up, expelled and recusancy fines were reintroduced.

Thus the stirrings of The Powder Treason began to be felt in the minds of some, not least Robert Catesby. Breaking point was reached when, on 24 April 1604, at James' request, a bill was introduced into the House of Commons. It classified all Roman Catholics as excommunicates, which meant that they could no longer make wills and dispose of their goods, making them, in effect, outlaws. No one need pay those debts or rents that they owed, and Catholics could not go to law or have the law's protection. They were to be considered as enemies of the state.

So, to teach them all a lesson, Robert Catesby, also known as the 'prince of darkness,' called a secret meeting with his fellow conspirators. The five core members of The Powder Treason, Robert Catesby, Thomas Wintour, John Wright, Thomas Percy and Guy Fawkes, met on Sunday 20 May 1604 at The Duck and Drake Inn in the Strand, London, to decide how to remove, with one blow, this odious man and his Parliament, along with a number of religious leaders. One of the reasons the plotters had for acting sooner rather then later was that they could not tolerate the newly-sanctioned version of the Bible, especially as it was going to be 'the best yet', for that would mean that the Roman Catholic cause would decline at a greater rate.

This must be stopped

Even though the plans were in an embryonic state, a number of the translators of this new version would also be present at the opening of Parliament, and they, too, would be soundly dealt with. Over three hundred people would have perished in the blast, including many relatives and friends of those original plotters meeting in the Strand. Contingency plans were also made, for if the king's son, Prince Charles, were not present with his father and elder brother, then he would have to be dealt with separately. One may wonder whether, many years later, King Charles (as he had become) mused on this irony at his trial in Westminster Hall, that he had been saved from death in Parliament in 1605, only to be executed at the wish of Parliament in Whitehall in 1649.

Parliament was due to meet again on 7 February 1605, just nine months away, so they would have to move speedily to get everything ready. After being persuaded by Catesby that this course of action was not only feasible but also right, the five core members swore on the prayer book that they would keep the plot a secret. They then moved into another room and, with Father John Gerard presiding, they celebrated the Roman Catholic Mass. It is unclear how much he knew about their plans at this time.

It is of more than passing significance that Guy Fawkes spent time in Roman Catholic Spain, and changed his name to Guido Fawkes. As in Elizabeth's reign, Spain was intimately involved in what was being planned for the overthrow of Protestant England.

The three Gs

The involvement of the Roman Catholic Society of Jesus, called the Jesuits, was assumed by many to be behind the plot, as they had previously organized, for Philip II, the Armada against Elizabeth I. A number of Jesuit priests have been associated with the plot, but three in particular—Father Henry Garnet, Father John Gerard and Father Oswald Greenway—have been considered as playing a prominent role in the proceedings.

FATHER HENRY GARNET

Garnet was born at Heanor in Derbyshire in 1555 and was educated at Winchester. A notable scholar, being an expert in Hebrew, Greek and Latin, for a time he became Professor of Hebrew at Rome. When James was travelling down from Scotland to claim the throne of England, Garnet was in a buoyant mood about the prospects of a new regime, for, as the superior of the Jesuits in England in 1587, he hoped to be influential in the new reign.

When James failed to live up to expectations, Garnet became typical of many Roman Catholic priests at that time, going about the country in secret, trying to remain undetected by the authorities. 'This secret life of priests living in hidden holes, squeezed into the gaps between walls and chimneys, lurking undetected in the dark within inches of those in the airy, well-lit rooms beside them, fuelled the vision of the Catholic as a man of darkness, his purpose unclear, his methods concealed, his whole existence dangerous.'[2]

To protect himself, he went by other names, 'Darcey, Meaze, Phillips, Walley, Roberts and Mr Farmer. He has achieved posthumous fame by being referred to by Shakespeare in *Macbeth*, Act 2, scene 3:

Porter. Here's a knocking, indeed! If a man were Porter of Hell Gate, he should have old turning the key. Knock, knock, knock. Who's there, i'th'name of Belzebub?—Here's a Farmer that hangd himself on th'expectation of plenty.

A little later in the play, he is referred to as an 'equivocator'. The first spectators would have been in no doubt in the minds of to whom Shakespeare was referring in his use of the term 'Mr Farmer', and the reason he did so.

It was said that Garnet was a master of equivocation, that is, speaking the truth to oneself while lying to someone else, and that many did not know when to trust his words.

FATHER JOHN GERARD

Gerard was involved in many activities before The Gunpowder Plot was thought of, and, as a result, he was captured in 1594 and taken to the Tower of London where he was severely tortured. Gerard made a dramatic escape from the Tower and was welcomed back into the Roman Catholic fold. He, too, went under a number of pseudonyms, and was known as 'Brooke, Lee, and Staunton'. It appears that he was ignorant of the existence of the plot because of his character, which caused Sir Everard Digby to say of him, 'it would not have been prudent to inform him'.

FATHER OSWALD GREENWAY

Otherwise known as Oswald Tesimond, or Tesmond, and sometimes Beaumont or Greenwell, he had been at school with Guy Fawkes in York. He was described as having a red complexion with black hair and beard. As a priest he travelled widely and was known to many, but he practised dissimulation when confronted by the authorities and held on to his beliefs secretly. He became a trusted confidant of Robert Catesby, but when Catesby revealed the plot in the confessional to Greenway, he told Garnet all about it. Therefore some have seen a weakness in him, as he was unable to respect the secret nature of the confessional.

Latin and the devil?

It is not too far fetched, as some have claimed, to see why the Jesuits, who were organized on military lines, would have been called upon to do something about the unruly situation in England. Many Roman Catholics would have been greatly disturbed about the prospect of a new translation of the Bible into English, for the control of the population by the priests could most effectively be undertaken through church services being conducted in Latin. Some said, rather sarcastically, that Latin was the right language for the Church because 'the devil could not understand it'!

However, Tyndale's famous statement about a ploughboy knowing more of the Scripture then a learned scholar was terrifying to them, because control of the population at large would be almost impossible if the mystical combined with the ritual of the priest was unmasked, and if simple faith in Jesus Christ was shown to be all that anyone needed for salvation.

Robert Cecil knew about these three Jesuits and, no doubt, his network of spies did their best to keep track of them and others as they travelled around the English countryside.

PHOTOGRAPH © ANDRE JENNY/PAINET INC.

The Twin Towers of the World Trade Center before 9/11

Terrorists plot

'Do not plot harm against your neighbour, who lives trustfully near you.'
Proverbs 3:29

James I had a great fear of assassination, for many a plot, real or imaginary, had been revealed to him. No doubt those who advised him, on occasions to suit their own purposes, would present a scenario to James that was designed, as it were, to scare the living daylights out of him. James had a mortal dread of gunpowder, as his father had been the victim of an explosion at his death.

Edinburgh

On the morning of 10 February 1567 at two o'clock, Lord Henry Darnley, father of James I, was killed, and the house in which he was staying. Kirk O' Field was destroyed by gunpowder. The explosion was so powerful that it awoke most of Edinburgh, and the side of the house was completely demolished. The bodies of Darnley and his page, Taylor, were found in their nightshirts; they had both been strangled or smothered before being blown out of the house.

Although James was only seven months old when his father died, the successive telling of the story left him with a mortal dread of gunpowder, but as his father had been blown from the house, it was assumed that the gunpowder had been placed *in* the house, and not *under* it. That is why the cellars of the Parliament House were not protected by guards in 1605, because no one thought that an attack would come from underneath where Parliament met.

Don't let them kill me

Another episode that etched itself onto James' mind occurred fifteen years later, in 1582. When he was sixteen years of age, an episode known as the Gowrie Plot made James permanently afraid of assassination. James had been out hunting—a favourite pastime of his—near Falkland in Scotland, when he was persuaded by Alexander, brother of the Earl of Gowrie, to ride over to Ruthven to interview a criminal who had been captured in Perth. At Gowrie's house he passed through various chambers which, rather suspiciously, were always locked after him, until he arrived in a small room where he was confronted by an armed man. In the ensuing struggle, James managed to cry out, 'Treason!' and his attendants fought their way in to rescue him. Gowrie and his brother Alexander were killed in the fighting. Poor James received the shock of his life, and afterwards always wore padded clothes to prevent a reoccurrence of being stabbed.

So to get near enough to deal with James, Catesby and his fellow conspirators would find it not only very difficult, but also extremely risky. They would have to prepare carefully if they were to fulfil their tainted mission.

The terrorists' triangle

The mode of operation known as 'The terrorists' triangle' can be perceived in the actions of the plotters in 1604–05, just as any terrorist group today. The three elements of this triangle are:

The Terrorist

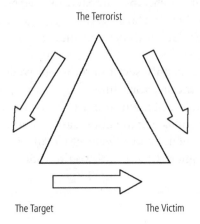

The Target   The Victim

Explanation of the triangle

A. FROM THE TERRORIST TO THE TARGET

A target is selected with the aim of achieving maximum effect, so that all who hear about the event are suitably shocked and become concerned about their own safety. Added to the sense of foreboding is the uncertainty from where or from whom the blow may come. It may have been the intention of one of the plotters to alarm James in this way when the Mounteagle letter was delivered (see Chapter 8).

B. FROM THE TERRORIST TO THE VICTIM

The terrorist tries to generate feelings of chronic fear in the intended victim so that he or she feels constantly under threat. The victim, in this case the English Protestant population, would have seen all their hopes go up in smoke and would have to realize that the gains of the English Reformation were going to be swept away.

C. FROM THE VICTIM TO THE TARGET

If James had died in the explosion, then it would be hoped that such a panic would ensue that the English would cry out for restoration to Rome, lest they, too, suffer horribly. The terrorists could then portray themselves as saviours ridding the country of a menace and bringing in a new order of peace and harmony.

New York City

On 11 September 2001 (9/11 as it is often referred to), the World Trade Center in New York City was hit by two aircraft flown by terrorists. Subsequently both towers collapsed. That was not the first time that the Twin Towers had been targeted, for, on 26 February 1993, a lorry that had been driven into a basement car park exploded, killing six and injuring over a thousand people. Consequently, the authorities did what they could to alleviate the chance of that happening again, for the terrorists had generated feelings of fear among the population at large. Measures were taken to ensure all vehicles entering the underground car park were inspected. What no one legislated for was an attack from the air; the terrorists had caused such panic and paranoia that it was assumed that if another attack took place, it had to be on the ground, so when the aircraft were flown into the buildings, everyone was taken by surprise.

James and his advisors would have been wary, but because his father had been blown out of a house, he did not ask the guard to look in the cellars of the Houses of Parliament as a routine matter of security. Everyone assumed that if an attack were to be made on him, it would come not from underneath him, but from alongside him.

In the name of God

Tragically, many acts of terrorism have been committed for religious reasons, and the most atrocious crimes have been perpetrated in the name of God, without a thought of the consequences for those who misuse his name. The commandments of God in Exodus 20:7 clearly state: 'You shall not misuse the name of the LORD your God, for the LORD will not hold anyone guiltless who misuses his name.' So all are warned against claiming divine approval for a plan when none has been given. God cannot be fooled, and his judgements do follow the wicked actions of men.

In New Testament times, Saul of Tarsus went around breathing out murderous threats against God's people—see Acts 9:1—and this must have been terrifying for them. However, God graciously met with him and changed him. In a frank and moving letter he tells his young friend, Timothy, what changed him, his attitude and beliefs: 'Even though I was once a blasphemer and a persecutor and a violent man, I was shown mercy because I acted in ignorance and unbelief. The grace of our Lord was poured out on me abundantly, along with the faith and love that are in Christ Jesus.' (1 Timothy 1:13–14). A similar miracle was needed by the plotters if they were to avoid making Paul's mistake. They may not have been granted a blinding light from heaven, but they did have access to God's Word through their priestly friends. This should have been a lamp for their feet and a light for their path (see Psalm 119:105).

Words into action

Instead, in June 1604, Catesby decided to see who else could be brought into the inner circle of plotters, as so much still needed to be done.

At the same time, Thomas Percy managed to hire lodgings close to Parliament House, and Guy Fawkes lived there, disguised as Percy's servant, using the name John Johnson. It is said that working in shifts, some of the plotters began digging a tunnel from that place, hoping it would end up bringing them right underneath their target. Some doubt the reality of this, saying the tunnel story is dubious, but something along these lines appeared originally to have happened, although it would have been quickly abandoned as unworkable. Guy Fawkes later said, while being tortured (so it may not have been true), that the walls may have been too thick to enable the work to progress smoothly. The tunnel become unsafe when water from the River Thames started to seep in, making the work very unpleasant and highly dangerous, and that project was thus abandoned.

It may be that this story was generated by Robert Cecil's spies to fuel popular belief in the devilish origin of the scheme, for a tunnel seemed to be in keeping with a design that was said to have been hatched in the depths of hell, and a picture of shadowy faces in a murky tunnel trying to accomplish a sinister deed was very alluring.

It was then announced on 23 December 1604 that Parliament would not open until October 1605, so this gave the plotters extra time to work on their scheme. In response to that statement, on 25 March 1605 they managed to lease a cellar directly beneath the House of Lords. This was so much easier as the House of Lords was situated on the first floor, and it meant the 'cellar' was, in fact, on the ground floor and was ideally situated for their purposes. This cellar had once been the old medieval kitchen of the Palace of Westminster and its previous occupant had stored coal in it. This gave it a suitably grubby feel and few noticed that there was even a cellar there.

Next on the agenda was the placing of thirty-six barrels of gunpowder into that cellar without arousing anyone's suspicion. Guy Fawkes arranged for it to be delivered from across the south bank of the Thames to the steps near Parliament, and then carried up into position. As there were many other businesses in the area that utilized barrels for their trade, this did not arose any suspicion, especially as it was done gradually between 25 March and 20 July 1605.

Why use gunpowder?

'Gunpowder is a simple but lethal concoction of three chemicals, ten per cent carbon, fifteen per cent sulphur and seventy-five per cent potassium nitrate or saltpetre. The nitrates in saltpetre produce oxygen, which expands on burning, creating an explosive reaction with carbon.' ... 'Saltpetre absorbs moisture from the air so, when left, gunpowder will go damp or "decay". This was the state the Gunpowder Plot powder was in.' Guy Fawkes 'did a dodgy deal and brought French gunpowder that was decayed. Each barrel would have held 100lbs. If his 3,600lbs of gunpowder had been fresh, it would have been enough to lay waste an area of Westminster with a radius of over 500 yards.'[1]

These barrels were carefully covered over with pieces of iron and billets of wood. When the gunpowder was eventually fired, these extra items would make deadly projectiles, thereby increasing the loss of life and injury to many. Many terrorists today include nails and other metal items in bombs, with exactly the same awful purpose in mind.

However, things were becoming increasingly difficult, and it was decided that even more people had to be involved in the plot. Robert Catesby drew others into the scheme. His servant, Thomas Bates, John Wright's brother, Christopher Wright, and Thomas Wintour all became involved in the proceedings.

Yet frustration was growing among the plotters because Parliament was delayed. The delay meant that Guy Fawkes was able to go back over to Flanders to seek additional support for the plot, and to obtain more gunpowder, as some had spoiled sitting in that damp cellar next to Parliament.

Trying to achieve such a task under the very noses of the enemy was fraught with danger, and although it is a matter of conjecture, it seems highly improbable that during this waiting period Robert Cecil's spies were still ignorant of what was taking place.

Secret confessions?

During July, Catesby met up with Father Greenway (Tesimond), and asked him to hear his confession. What he told Greenway was so unexpected and dramatic that the priest was in a quandary as to what to do about it, for Catesby confessed to him the details of his proposed plot. According to Roman Catholic dogma, confession is always completely secret, and, by the rules of the 'seal of the confessional', the priest must never tell anyone else. So, in seeking absolution for his sin, Catesby felt secure in the knowledge that what he had confessed would never be known to another soul. Greenway was rightly appalled by what he heard, and could see the implications of such a plot devised by these extremists. It seemed highly probable to him that when the plot failed, not only would many people be implicated, not least the Jesuits, but also all the Catholics of England would suffer great hardship and maybe even death as a result.

What could the troubled priest do? After worrying about it, a simple solution came to him; he went and visited Father Garnet, the leader of his order, and asked him to hear his confession. Now Garnet was also drawn in and became associated with what was being planned, but what could he do to stop the folly of these men? Apart from the full complement of priests in England confessing to one another, there was no other way to make it known, and then, of course, playing by the 'rules', the priests could still not tell anyone else. The foolishness of the confessional was only too apparent. It was wrong, for it went against the plain teaching of the Bible as well as common decency. Even though he knew about the plot, Garnet was still prepared to watch many die a horrible death rather then speak up and stop such an occurrence, lest he fall into trouble with his superiors for going against Church teaching.

Although he did seek a way out of the dilemma, he now found himself locked in it. Hoping to save his skin and not to break the seal of the confessional, he sent messages to Rome, hinting that something cruel was being intended, hoping that the Pope would speak out against the violence planned—but there was little likelihood of this!

Time on their hands

The days dragged on into weeks and all that was left for the plotters to do was to wait for the reassembling of Parliament. It was then announced, on 28 July, that Parliament would now not open until 5 November. It seemed that the new order was taking for ever to commence. While Fawkes was away in August 1605, Catesby decided, after speaking to some of the others at Bath, to organize yet further support. Whether he did this out of necessity or out of shear bravado, it is difficult to tell, but John Grant, Sir Everard Digby, Robert Keyes, Ambrose Rookwood and, maybe fatally for the plotters, Catesby's cousin, Francis Tresham, were added to their number over the next few months, making a total of thirteen. Maybe this course of action was decided upon because of the delay in Parliament's opening, but they could also see a number of areas that needed dealing with which were beyond the few of them currently involved.

At last the autumn came with all in place. They had gone over their plans meticulously several times and were determined to leave nothing to chance. It had been decided that Guy Fawkes would light the fuse and be safely across the River Thames when the gunpowder ignited. With all haste he would then get to a ship that would transport him across the English Channel to Flanders where those he had sought to rally to the cause would be invited to join an invasion army to bring the English back under the rule of Rome. Meanwhile, many of the others would be overseeing the uprising in the Roman Catholic stronghold of the Midlands, including the capture of the young Princess Elizabeth, who would become their puppet monarch. However, against all the odds, an unexpected and controversial event took place. A letter was delivered on a dark night by a dark visitor, with a dark purpose in mind …

Ightham Mote

5/11

'Do not envy a violent man or choose any of his ways, for the LORD detests a perverse man but takes the upright into his confidence.' Proverbs 3:31–32

O n Saturday evening 26 October 1605, after serving dinner, Thomas Ward, a servant, was taking the air outside the Hoxton residence of Lord Mounteagle in the north of London when, out of the shadows, a tall dark stranger, cloaked with a hat pulled over the eyes, approached and gave him a letter. Without waiting or saying anything, this person, assumed to be a man, turned and disappeared into the gathering gloom, never to be seen again.

The servant took the letter to his master, who, in turn, handed it on to another person to read. Some see in this a sinister ploy, and that Mounteagle knew in advance what the letter contained and wanted others who were dining with him to know its contents. Maybe that is just too fanciful and the real reason he passed it to another person was simply because his hands were soiled from eating his meal.

The letter warned him in stark language not to go to the House of Lords for the opening of Parliament. The surviving letter is preserved in the public records office and appears to be written with red ink, perhaps to convey the urgency of its message as well as a stark warning about the carnage to come.

The letter reads:

My Lord, out of the love I bear to some of your friends, I have a care of your preservation, therefore I advise you as you tender your life to devise some excuse to shift your attendance at this parliament, for God and man have concurred to punish the wickedness of this time, and think not slightly of this advertisement, but retire yourself into your country, where you may expect the event in safety, for though there be no appearance of any stir, yet I say they shall receive a terrible blow this parliament and yet they shall not see who hurts them, this counsel is not to be condemned because it may do you good and can do you no harm, for the danger is past as soon as you have burnt the letter and I hope God will give you the grace to make good use of it, to whose holy protection I commend you.

Was it a genuine warning or a 'put-up' job? That letter seems too detailed, as though it had to convey to others, besides Mounteagle, plainly and clearly what was going to happen. The dramatic result of this letter was catastrophic for the plotters, because the hunters were soon to become the hunted as Mounteagle hastened off to show it to Robert Cecil in Whitehall, central London. Around the same time, Thomas Ward, Lord Mounteagle's servant who had been given that letter, sent a message of warning to Robert Catesby. He knew that Catesby was friendly with Christopher Wright whose sister was Ward's wife, so he had a vested family interest in warning his brother-in-law Wright. He told Catesby that Mounteagle had been tipped off about an event at the next opening of Parliament.

Whose side are you on?
Lord Mounteagle is a fascinating character, and it is a strong possibility that he was a double agent and really in the employ of Robert Cecil.

On his birth, he was named William Parker. He came from a family with a strong Roman Catholic background. His father was Baron Moreley and his mother was the daughter and heiress of the third Lord Mounteagle; her son would eventually come into both titles.

William Parker was married in 1589 to Elizabeth Tresham, the younger sister of Francis Tresham who was also involved in the plot. He was involved in the abortive Essex rebellion against Queen Elizabeth in 1601, and only escaped the execution block by writing a letter to Robert Cecil declaring his innocence of any intended overthrow of her majesty, and by making the subsequent payment of a fine of £8,000. It is possible that, at this stage in his life, he became, under Cecil's tutelage, a government spy.

When James I became king, this saw a rise in Mounteagle's star and he gained a seat in the House of Lords, dangerously close to Guy Fawkes' store of gunpowder.

He was close to Catesby, whom he referred to as 'Dear Robin', and, in July 1605, held a meeting with him at which Francis Tresham and Father Garnet were also present. He might also have met up with Robert Catesby and Thomas Percy at Bath in September 1605. So he was well in with both camps, and, in many ways, would have made an ideal conspirator, but something stopped Catesby from drawing him into the inner workings of the thirteen plotters, even though they had been involved in several other schemes. Did they suspect that he was not all that he appeared to be, and therefore kept him at a distance?

Whatever the truth might be, Mounteagle was worried that he might be implicated in any fall-out from an event, and so he rushed off to Robert Cecil, the most powerful man in England under James. There was no one better placed to unravel the letter's hidden meaning than Sir Robert Cecil, Earl of Salisbury, who was a brilliant and cunning politician. He read the letter with great interest, for his spies had warned him that the Roman Catholics were up to something. This seemed to be the final piece of the jigsaw he had been putting together.

King James was hunting deer in Essex, and so he was not shown the letter until Friday 1 November and, playing as it did on his fear of assassination, it immediately drew a response from him. The King believed that something to do with gunpowder was being referred to: '... they shall receive a terrible blow this parliament and yet they shall not see who hurts them', and that could only mean an explosion, couldn't it? So, over the next few days, Cecil put into place a number of measures that would determine the extent of the threat, and the Parliament building would be searched for any threatening material.

Did you write it?

Many theories abounded as to the origin of that letter. One unusual one came about with a gruesome find at Ightham Mote, an old manor house a few miles from Tonbridge in Kent. In Victorian times, a workman carrying out essential repairs discovered a human skeleton that had apparently been deliberately bricked up behind a wall.

The house belonged to a Roman Catholic family, that of the Selbys, and, it seems (or so the story goes) that Dorothy Selby, a young woman, had fallen in love with Lord Mounteagle. She had overheard the details of the plot, and, realizing that Lord Mounteagle would be attending the sitting of Parliament on 5 November, in desperation she wrote the letter to warn him.

So, when the plot failed, she may have been blamed and therefore have paid a terrible price for her love by being bricked up alive.

However, this theory is based on circumstantial evidence rather than hard fact. Dame Dorothy Selby died in 1641, thirty-six years after the event, so, unless someone had a long memory, it is highly unlikely that she was the one walled up at Ightham Mote. One reason for this theory is the third monument in Ightham Church, which, it is claimed, links Dorothy Selby with the letter that betrayed the plotters.

The inscription to her in the church reads:

> She was a Dorcas
> Whose curious needle turned the abused stage
> Of this lewd World into the golden age:
> Whose pen of steel and silken ink enrolled
> The acts of Jonah in records of gold;
> Whose art disclosed that plot, which had it taken;
> Rome had triumphed and Britain's walls had shaken;
> She was
> In heart, a Lydia; and in tongue, a Hanna,
> In Zeal a Ruth; in wedlock a Susanna.
> Prudently simple, providently wary;
> To the world a Martha: and to heaven a Mary.

This is fulsome praise indeed, and her skill as a Dorcas—a needlewoman referred to Acts 9:39—is shown in plaster on the monument on which her epitaph appears. The legend that she was involved in the discovery of the plot is based on a misunderstanding of the words in the inscription, 'whose art disclosed the plot', which did not mean that she had overheard and betrayed the plot, but actually meant that she had depicted it in her tapestry work. Any other construction on those words needs a greater basis then mere speculation.

This leaves the intriguing question, if they aren't those of Dame Dorothy Selby, then whose remains did the Victorian workman actually discover?

At the time of the plot, it seems that the favourite choice for the author of that letter is the last of the plotters to join, Francis Tresham, who was related not only to Lord Mounteagle, but also to Catesby and the Wright brothers. So incensed and sure of their facts were Catesby and Tom Wintour that they were going to hang Tresham, but he swore his innocence with such vehemence that the pair left him alone.

Lady Antonia Fraser argues for the author of the letter to be none other than Mounteagle along with Robert Cecil, who, knowing of the plot's existence, revealed it to the world in this fashion. It is a fact that James I gave Lord Mounteagle an annuity of £500 for life, and also lands which were worth £200 each year, a considerable sum of money in those days, and this would have helped in making up the shortfall in his finances after that £8,000 fine in 1601.

Whatever the truth may be, as a result of that letter—before King James had seen it—on Wednesday 30 October 1605, Guy Fawkes was spotted going into a cellar in Westminster. He wanted to make sure the gunpowder was still in place, and that all was ready for the big day. Maybe he had become complacent, but he did not realize that he had been seen. No doubt Robert Cecil's spies, if not directly involved, would have been alerted, and, as a consequence, the days of Fawkes and the other plotters were numbered.

On Sunday evening 3 November, Thomas Percy, having arrived back in London, met with Catesby and Wintour. He found that Francis Tresham had suspiciously been putting pressure on them to abandon the plot and flee because of the Mounteagle letter. The sensible thing to do would have been to call the whole thing off and melt away into the autumn mist, but Catesby and Percy were determined, cost what it may, to see the venture through.

Into action

At about 11am on Monday 4 November, Thomas Percy called on his relative, the Catholic Earl of Northumberland, saying that he wanted to discover if there were any rumours of a plot circulating among James's court officials. He was relived to find none.

Later that day around 5pm, Thomas Percy met up with fellow conspirators Robert Keyes, Thomas Wintour and John (Jack) Wright to tell them that all was well, before going off to his lodgings to prepare for an early morning escape from London. Near this time, Lords Mounteagle and Suffolk, along with a few other people, casually inspected the cellar beneath the House of Lords. Close by stood a tall man—Fawkes—but they pretended not to notice, and they left as though everything was normal and of little concern to them.

After taking what he thought were sufficient precautions, Guy Fawkes met up with Robert Keyes at 10pm to collect a watch that Catesby had left for him; he needed it to time the fuse that would set off the gunpowder. Meanwhile, Robert Catesby rode out heading for the Midlands, where he would play a prominent role in the forthcoming uprising.

Everything seemed to be going according to plan, but then it all unravelled. At midnight or in the small hours of Tuesday 5 November, a second and more thorough search party returned to the area of the cellar beneath the House of Lords. King James had sent them with express orders to be most thorough in their investigations. In a corner of the infamous cellar, they discovered a figure in a dark hat and cloak, booted and spurred as though for rapid flight, carrying a lantern. After a struggle, he was apprehended by Sir Thomas Knevett and the other members of the search party. The supposed lantern has ended up in the Tradescant Room of the Ashmolean Museum in Oxford, where it can still be seen.

Having been caught fast, Guy Fawkes was now frisked, and it was discovered that he had all the tools on him necessary to fire the gunpowder, together with the watch he had picked up that afternoon. He boldly said to his captors that had he been able to, he would have fired the gunpowder and blown all of them, including himself, up. Yet he would not have succeeded, for, as has already been seen, the gunpowder was so old and had been in place so long that it would not have exploded. All their efforts had been for nothing! The news of the foiling of the desperate plot spread like wildfire all over London.

In the year 2002, a newsflash stated that Guy Fawkes' gunpowder had been found. This was certainly a headline to capture people's attention; however, on closer inspection, it has to be treated with caution. The statement read: 'Experts have found a bar of gunpowder in the British Library Cellar that *might have been used* (my italics) by Guy Fawkes when he tried to destroy Parliament in 1605. A collection of different kinds of gunpowder dating back hundreds of years was given to the museum in 1995, but it's taken them this long to get to this particular bar. The gunpowder was given to the library among other papers belonging to a seventeenth-century writer called John Evelyn. His family made lots of money a very long time ago from making gunpowder.'[1]

Christopher Wright, hearing that Fawkes had been taken, went as speedily as he could to alert Thomas Wintour and Thomas Percy, saying that London was now no longer safe for them. Percy and Wright left London quickly and, as he left, Percy said to his servant, William Talbois, 'I am undone.' Shortly after, Robert Keyes left and then some time after him, Ambrose Rookwood, saddling his horse, rode off at great pace. He was probably the best horseman among the plotters and covered thirty miles in two hours. He finally caught up with Thomas Bates, Robert Catesby and John Wright in Bedfordshire, telling them that Fawkes had been captured and the plot had failed.

Showing great courage, Thomas Wintour remained in London and decided to see if the news was as bad as first thought. He went down to Westminster, and saw that the guards were stopping and questioning people. A stranger turned to him and said: 'There is treason discovered in which the King and the Lords were to be blown up.' He realized that he was in great danger, so he rode off, heading towards his brother's house at Huddington in Worcestershire.

To the Tower

All this frenetic activity on the part of the plotters was possible because one of their number was holding fast against enormous pressure, for that very tall and desperate fellow who had been apprehended and bound fast showed incredible courage when questioned, giving his name as 'John Johnson, servant to Master Thomas Percy'. Because he had spent so much time abroad, Fawkes was unknown to Cecil's spies. So they lead him before the Privy Council and then, in the early hours of the morning, to the King, where he confessed openly that he was going to blow up Parliament House. James questioned him as to his motive and was given the answer that his intention 'was to blow the beggarly Scots back to their native mountains'. Maybe some of the Council suppressed smiles at this statement, for a number of James' retinue from Scotland had made themselves very unpopular in London, because of their speech, ways, habits, and their perceived greed.

Frustrated by the lack of answers to his questions, James handed Fawkes over to a strong guard, who ferried him on the River Thames from Westminster to the Tower of London. Passing through Traitors' Gate and into the hands of the Lieutenant was the signal to Fawkes of the end of his freedom. The Lieutenant was given permission to use all appropriate means to extract not only a full confession but also to get the names of others who must have been in on the plot. It should be mentioned that in 1215, the Magna Carta, that cornerstone of English liberties, expressly forbids torture.

Later at Fawkes' trial, the prosecuting council, Sir Edward Coke (who would have known this by skilful manipulation of language) said that 'just helpful persuasions had been used'.

The hated enemy of the English, the Spanish Inquisition (also known as The Holy Office) employed torture, and, ironically, this was one of the aspects which aroused horror among the English, especially the merchants who did not want to be caught during the reign of Elizabeth I. It was also a spur in trying to keep that vast Armada from landing in England and bringing the Inquisition's tortures into the land.

Whatever the law says, for those in power there is always a way around it. Kept in the public records office, the following letter, written by James I to his council regarding the interrogation of Guy Fawkes, concludes with the following instructions: 'If he will not otherwise confess, the gentler tortures are to be first used on him, and so by degrees until the ultimate is reached, and so God speed your work—James R' Guy Fawkes had been taken to the Tower of London, a fate that, since Tudor times, had conjured up images of the worst sort. He was interrogated in the Council Chamber in the Queen's House before being placed in a narrow and dark cell. For some of his confinement, he may have been in 'Little ease', which was so small that a man could neither stand up nor stretch out, and, as a consequence, the prisoner would suffer great pain.

It is also just possible that he may have been incarcerated for a period of time in the Salt Tower, which has particular associations with Jesuit sufferers in the sixteenth and seventeenth centuries. The monogram, IHS, with a cross above the H, a device commonly used by the Society of Jesus, occurs several times among the carvings on the walls of the stone chambers.

Fawkes continued insisting that he was John Johnson and, incredibly, considering his situation, he maintained this name for forty-eight hours, until, broken under torture, he confessed that his name was really Guido Fawkes. The usual place for torture was the ground floor of the White Tower, although some think it may have been in the basement of the Wakefield Tower. It is not known for sure what 'processes' Guy Fawkes had to endure, but probably they included the infamous rack, which was known as the 'Duke of Exeter's daughter', because the fourth Duke of Exeter had introduced it in the fifteenth century. Another apparatus that was a favourite of the operators was the 'Scavenger's daughter', for, unlike the rack, this one was portable and could visit people wherever they were lodged. This device was introduced during the reign of Henry VIII, and although appearing deceptively simple, it was more feared then the rack because of the extreme agonies it inflicted. No one could hold out for very long when were placed in it and the screw was tightened.[2]

In 1605, the Tower of London was also a zoo. In 1604, James had called upon one of the Masters of the Royal Game, in charge of the Mastiff Dogs, to procure good fighting dogs to test the courage of his newly acquired African Lion. So it is just possible in November 1605 that, above the roar of beasts, the agonized cries of Guy Fawkes could be heard as the interrogators set to work on him. When at last Fawkes confessed, all he said was, 'It was the devil and not God who was the discoverer of the plot.'

But what of the others?

While Guy Fawkes was enduring great torment, the others, frightened for their lives, were to be found in the Midlands. On the evening of 5 November, Robert Catesby, Thomas Bates, Thomas Percy, Ambrose Rookwood and the Wright brothers were joined by Sir Everard Digby and Robert Wintour with various other Catholics, numbering about fifty in total. However, as they rode through the night, some who had only been on the periphery of the plot melted away into the darkness; they did not have the stomach to face the fight that must come.

The others met up with Thomas Wintour at Huddington and decided on 6 November, in pouring rain, to ride onto Holbeach House, the Staffordshire home of one of the Catholics that Digby had recruited.

However, a great mistake had been made on their journey north, for some of them broke into the stables at Warwick Castle and stole horses; this foolish act alerted those who were after them as to their exact whereabouts. It was believed that the group were heading for refuge in Wales. But that thoughtless theft meant the High Sheriff of Worcestershire, Sir Richard Walsh, was by now aware of their location and was in hot pursuit with over two hundred men riding to apprehend the plotters. It was all so hopeless.

With the resolve of the group sapping away, and with their morale as grey as the skies, Sir Everard Digby then left the group going off to surrender to the authorities and plead for mercy. Then, to compound their problems, another unforeseen incident caused the remaining conspirators to lose heart even more. At Holbeach House, a strange and most ironic thing occurred: for some peculiar reason, those who had gathered there decided to dry out some gunpowder that had become damp in the rain, and so, very foolishly, they put it in front of an open fire! If they had been in their right mind, they would have quickly realized just how unwise such an action was. The inevitable happened: a spark from the fire ignited the gunpowder and there was an explosion. Four of them were hurt, Robert Catesby and Ambrose Rookwood suffered injuries, but John Grant's face was disfigured—indeed, he was almost blinded. So, they had their explosion, but not as they had intended it. Robert Wintour became unnerved by this event and spoke of a terrible dream that he had had in which this catastrophe was pictured to him and in it he recognized the finger of Almighty God which was against them. For him, this was the last straw. Not able to take any more, he left in the rain, soon to be followed by Thomas Bates who slipped away when it became dark.

Those who remained behind did not have long to wait for the government forces to arrive on Friday 8 November. The plotters decided that all they could do was die, but not without a final show of resistance. The assault started with the authorities deciding to smoke them out, and, in the confusion of the smoke and the gunfight, Thomas Wintour was shot in the arm, then Christopher and John Wright were hit (these two died soon after of their wounds). Ambrose Rookwood was wounded, and, along with some others, was captured.

Last stand of the conspirators

Meanwhile, in shades of what would happen to Butch Cassidy and the Sundance kid in the nineteenth century, the three plotters, Robert Catesby, Thomas Percy and Thomas Wintour, stood together just inside the door, and then moved outside to face the guns in a final shoot-out, clinging hopelessly to their older version of English religion. It was said that Catesby and Percy died as a result of a single shot fired by John Streete of Worcester that passed through Percy's body and into Catesby. Percy was killed instantly, but Catesby crawled back inside the house to die, and he was found holding on to a picture of the Virgin Mary. Later, according to Father Gerard, Catesby said that 'not for themselves but for the cause of Christ, not for their wives but for the Church, the spouse of Christ, and saving so many thousand souls, the children of God, from eternal flames, they attempted with fire to cut off the chiefest heads and only causes of that greater ruin'. Although it is not improbable that he said words to that effect, it does seem highly unlikely that, in the heat of a gun fight and its aftermath, anyone took accurate note of his final utterances.

Thomas Bates was arrested in Staffordshire, Robert Keyes was caught, and Sir Everard Digby eventually gave himself up on 10 November, while Robert Wintour, along with another Catholic, Stephen Littleton, remained on the run until 9 January 1606 when their hiding place was betrayed by a cook.

Francis Tresham, who many thought was responsible for the Mounteagle letter, was arrested in London on 12 November, but he did not come to trial, for in the Tower of London, in a poor state of health, his condition worsened until he died of an unspecified urethral infection. Some people said he had been poisoned in order to stop him telling the full story and implicating both Robert Cecil and Lord Mounteagle.

A merciful monarch?

While all this was taking place, James I calmly gave a speech to Parliament on Saturday 9 November, using the occasion to wax lyrical about the events of that week. He was in a magnanimous mood, saying that he would show himself merciful towards English Catholics who had not been involved in the plot. Although many prominent Catholic members of society were closely questioned, with Sir Walter Raleigh denying any connection with the plot, he was in an especially difficult position, as his wife, Elizabeth Throckmorton, was a first cousin of Lady Catesby.

Subsequently, the foiling and capturing of the conspirators was seen by Protestants as God's gracious intervention in the affairs of men, and it was often recalled as an example of evil that should never be forgotten, and principally as the revealing of the mercy of God rather than the revealing of the mercy of James.

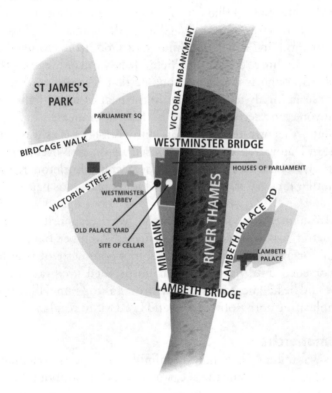

The area inside the circle would have been affected by the blast from 36 barrels of gunpowder
Note: the shaded area shows the estimated extent of the blast. Westminster and Lambeth bridges shown in this map would not have been there in the seventeenth century

Unfit to live

'The LORD's curse is on the house of the wicked, but he blesses the home of the righteous.' Proverbs 3:33

J ustice not only had to be done, but had to be seen to be done. Robert Cecil was not very keen on pursuing too many Catholics lest it have a detrimental effect. It was, after all, only fifty years previously that Mary I had acted in unremitting fashion, which was to give her the sobriquet 'Bloody Mary'. Alienating the population at large was a dangerous path to follow, so only those who could be shown to be traitors to the crown would be hunted down and severely dealt with.

From Cecil's standpoint, the major threat came from the Jesuits, as they were run along semi-military lines, and were dedicated to spreading Roman Catholicism. Here was an ideal opportunity to crush that religious order.

Torture, used skilfully, can give almost perfect results, or so it was thought. After another excruciating session of interrogation on 9 November, Guy Fawkes had named Father John Gerard as having given the Mass to the plotters in The Duck and Drake Inn back on 20 May 1604, and this was after they had sworn an oath of secrecy regarding the plot. Thomas Wintour, on 23 November, also gave the name, Father John Gerard. Then, on 29 November, Francis Tresham named Father Henry Garnet, and this was followed on 4 December by Thomas Bates giving the name of Father Oswald Greenway (Tesimond). Then another confession was forthcoming from Bates, this time on 13 January 1606, when he named all three, Fathers Garnet, Gerard and Greenway.

Wanted, dead or alive

Robert Cecil had all he needed, and on 15 January a proclamation was issued for the capture of these three men, with special attention being given to Garnet, as he was the leader of the English Jesuits. His description was provided as being: 'full faced, fat of body, of complexion fair, his forehead high on each side with a little hair thinning down.' On the day of the proclamation, Father Greenway, fleeing for his life, boarded a ship and escaped to the Continent hiding in a cargo of dead pigs.

Garnet had fled to Hindlip Hall in Worcestershire, thinking that he could remain hidden in one of the many priest holes. A priest hole was a small hiding place that would, it was hoped, enable the priest to escape detection when the 'Poursuivants' called looking for them.

Garnet had gone to a known Catholic safe house, so it was not long before the government agents turned up to search for him. Had they received a tip-off? Certainly the search was extensive, lasting from 20 to 27 January 1606 when Garnet, along with another priest, Father Oldcorne, could hold out no longer, despite the obvious presence of their enemies. The main problem was that there were no facilities in their small priest hole, and the stench of their own waste matter had become overpowering.

These two were transported back and placed in adjoining cells in the Tower of London, which had a small opening passing between them so that the two prisoners could talk to each other. Maybe their recent experiences had dulled their minds, for they did not realize the obvious, that another small opening also ran from their cells, and Cecil's men could hear all that they said to each other.

Transcripts of Garnet's interrogations survive in the public records office at Kew, and show how he tried to avoid telling what he knew. Part of one reads: 'Were you not asked by Catesby for some great attempt, either by gunpowder or otherwise, for the Catholic cause? How say you, Mr Garnet, did Mr Tresham equivocate or no?'

'I know not,' was his answer.

Father Oldcorne was executed with others in April, but Henry Garnet was left until 5 May 1606, when he died the traitor's death in the Churchyard of St Paul's. Some of the straw which lay under his remains became spotted with blood, and some superstitiously saw an image of the dead priest on it. This was smuggled out of England, but vanished at the time of the French Revolution. The day of Garnet's execution saw Gerard also in great fear of capture, disguised as a servant to a party of foreign envoys escaping to the Continent.

The fate of the conspirators

The eight plotters, Thomas Bates, Sir Everard Digby, Guy Fawkes, John Grant, Robert Keyes, Ambrose Rookwood, Robert and Thomas Wintour were in an unenviable position. Their show trial was held on 27 January 1606, in the ancient Westminster Hall, which still stands in the Parliament complex, and where many famous people like Winston Churchill and Queen Elizabeth the Queen Mother have laid in state before their funeral services. This great hall is situated only a short distance away from the cellar that had been the centre of so much activity; the plotters had been so near and yet were now so far from what they had hoped to achieve. These eight surviving conspirators were put on show and forced to stand on a raised platform so that all could see them. King James watched the proceedings from a private room.

In the indictment that was read out at the start of the trial, the Jesuit Fathers, Garnet, Gerard and Greenway, were all mentioned as being participators in the plot. The men standing before the court were charged with trying to:

Deprive the King of his crown;

Murder King, Queen, and Prince;

Stir rebellion and sedition in the kingdom;

Bring miserable destruction amongst the subjects;

Change, alter and subvert the religion here established;

Ruinate the state of the commonwealth, and to bring strangers to invade it.

The counsel for the crown was Sir Edward Coke and Sir Edward Philips, whereas the prisoners had no representation, and all of the plotters, except Sir Everard Digby, pleaded 'not guilty'. They were questioned as to why they had entered such a plea when their guilt was beyond doubt. Guy Fawkes, seemingly answering for all, said that he had done so 'in respect of certain conferences mentioned in the indictment' which he said that he 'knew not of [and] which were answered to have been set down according to course of law, as necessarily presupposed before the resolution of such a design'.

Sir Everard Digby, who had many friends present at his trial, said to the Lords in attendance, 'If I but hear any of your Lordships forgive me, I shall go more cheerfully to the gallows.' The Lords replied, 'God forgive you, and we do.'

Coincidentally, on the same day as the trial, 27 January 1606, the Jesuit priest, Father Henry Garnet, was captured and brought back to London.

A punishment to fit the crime?

In the United Kingdom today, whenever a terrible crime comes to light, calls for the death penalty to be reinstated are heard in many places. Bible-believing Christians are not always united on this issue, but for the people of the seventeenth century the subject was not open to debate, for in the Bible (Romans 13:1–5), God had clearly spelt out the role of rulers to maintain justice. As the famous twentieth-century preacher Martyn Lloyd-Jones said,

It seems to me that, based on the teaching here, [Romans 13] the argument for the death penalty can be put like this: capital punishment is designed to maintain and to emphasize and to establish the sanctity of life. It has no vindictive quality in it at all. If the vindictive element comes in, it is wrong. The purpose of capital punishment is not to say, 'You have taken someone's life, I am going to take yours.' It is not that at all. The purpose of capital punishment is to vindicate God's lordship over life, and to tell man that if he passes beyond that border, he must forfeit his own life. There is nothing that should teach us the sacredness and the sanctity of life as the carrying out of capital punishment.[1]

They had not taken any lives but had, in the eyes of the law, committed treason and it meant that they could not escape and were duly condemned as traitors. Whatever the nature of their crime, they did not deserve to face the horror prepared for them. Like others before them, they could have been imprisoned for life. Desperate times, however, are often accompanied by desperate measures, so for this high treason it was decreed that the condemned should be taken from their prison to a place of execution, to be hanged, drawn and quartered. This terrible sentence was to be inflicted on the victims, because in a brutal age it was felt that a quick blow from an axe formed no deterrent to other traitors, who, perhaps, were plotting equally terrible things.

The official wording in 1606 stated specifically:

They shall be drawn backward at a horse's tail, with the head declining downwards, and lying so near the ground as may be practical, for they are unfit to benefit of common air.

They shall be strangled being hung by the neck between heaven and earth as deemed unworthy of both.

Then cut down alive and have their privy parts cut off and burnt before their faces, as being unworthily begotten, and unfit to leave any generation after them.

Their bowels and inlay parts to be taken out and burnt, and then the head is to be cut off, and lastly the body quartered and the quarters set up in some high and eminent place to the view and detestation of men, and to become prey for the fowls of the air.

This dreaded punishment was only abolished on 4 July 1870.

Fun for all?

Public executions used to be high points in the dull life of many an ordinary citizen, and they compare with the bloodlust of the Roman amphitheatres, where many people suffered appallingly for the gratification of the baying crowd. It is as though the death of others would somehow spare the onlooker from its power. As the centrepiece of the attractions, gross indignities were experienced by the condemned to heighten the crowd's fervour and horror.

Two executioners, Derrick and his assistant Gregory Brandon—who in 1649 beheaded Charles I—probably carried out the butchery on the unfortunate sufferers. Derrick has subsequently given his name to the crane, shaped like a gibbet, that is still used to offload goods at docksides.

The dazed and bruised victims were brought to the scaffold and normally they would say something while the final preparations were made. Then the condemned person would be hanged by the neck. Unlike in the case of modern methods where the neck is broken swiftly at the end of a long drop, these men endured the agony of slow strangulation, as the short drop method was employed. The effects of this on the human body were degrading with the loss of control for both bladder and bowels, but, instead of sympathy, this often brought great amusement to the crowd, who delighted in the sufferings of such terrible criminals.

The executioner usually cut the victims down before death occurred and, if they had passed out, revived them, if he could, for the next stage—the drawing. The genitals were removed and burned in front of them, then the abdomen was sliced open and the intestines were extracted, and also burned. Normally this was the point when the victim died of shock. But the crowd was waiting for the climax, where, like a grizzly trophy, the heart was removed and held aloft. As the heart is a muscle, it can beat for up to half an hour after brain-death and so the executioner could be covered with blood as the cheers went up. Then the corpse was beheaded and quartered and the remains taken away to be fixed to some appropriate landmark as a warning to other would-be traitors.

Old St Paul's

The unfortunates were sometimes stripped before being tied to a wooden hurdle, face up with the feet towards the horse's tail, to show how low they had sunk. Many times the public were able to sport with the victims by throwing refuse or dung at them or striking out with a stick to show their displeasure. After enduring such treatment on Thursday 30 January 1606, Sir Everard Digby, Robert Wintour, John Grant and Thomas Bates ascended the scaffold that had been constructed at the western end of St Paul's Churchyard, not far from the place where members of the Royal Family disembark from their cars or carriages when they now visit the Cathedral. The site was described as being 'over and against the Bishop of London's house'. This was outside the old cathedral that was subsequently burnt down in the great fire of London in 1666. The location of the scaffold was probably very deliberately chosen, because it was near here that Queen Elizabeth I had come to thank God for her nation's deliverance from the Armada, and now these men would die so that the people could again be thankful that, yet again, a Spanish Jesuit Catholic plan had been foiled.

On his final journey, Thomas Bates' wife, Martha, managed to break through the guards and throw herself onto the hurdle carrying her husband, and he took the opportunity to tell her where he had hidden the £100 which had been given to him by Christopher (Kit) Wright for his family. When he ascended the scaffold, he appeared to be completely penitent and said that affection for his master—Robert Catesby—caused him to forget his duty to God, his king and country. He asked for forgiveness and died with such courage that he surprised many.

John Grant had to be led to the scaffold as the injuries sustained when the gunpowder blew up at Holbeach House had virtually blinded him. He was asked if he was sorry for his actions and replied, saying it was 'not the time nor the place to discuss cases of conscience'. He had come there to die, 'not to dispute matters of that kind'. He also said he was 'convinced that our project was far from being sinful'.

Poor Sir Everard Digby, despite the Lords' forgiveness at his trial, was hung for a very short time and went to the quartering block, undoubtedly still alive. Cecil's cousin, Sir Francis Bacon, told the highly improbable story that when the executioner removed Digby's heart and held it aloft saying, 'Here is the heart of a traitor,' Digby responded, 'Thou liest.'

Now to Westminster

The next day, Friday 31 January 1606, Thomas Wintour, Ambrose Rookwood, Robert Keyes and Guy Fawkes undertook a similar journey but their destination was Old Palace Yard, Westminster, very close to where the monarch disembarks from the state coach at the state opening of Parliament. Again, the location was deliberately chosen so that in 'that very place, which they had planned to demolish in order to hammer home the message of their wickedness,' they would suffer and die.

While being dragged to his execution, Ambrose Rookwood called out to his wife in the Strand, 'Pray for me, pray for me.' Elizabeth replied, 'I will, and be of good courage. Offer thyself wholly to God. I, for my part, do as freely restore thee to God as he gave thee unto me.' And he was gone.

Arriving at the site of the scaffold he made a speech and prayed that, 'God would make the King a catholic.' It is said that the crowd were moved to tears because he been well known and loved. His speech and deportment earned him mercy, as he was hanged until almost dead, suffering less than his fellow conspirators.

An eyewitness of these events on that January day wrote: 'Last of all came the great devil of all, Guy Fawkes, alias Johnson, who should have put fire to the powder. His body being weak with torture and sickness he was scarce able to go up the ladder, yet with much ado, by the help of the hangman went up high enough to break his neck in the fall. He made no speech, but with crosses and idle ceremonies made his end upon the gallows and the block, to the great joy of all the beholders that the land was ended of so wicked a villainy.'

After the carnage the crowds went back to business or to their homes, but England was never the same. Just forty-five years later, another scaffold was constructed up the road in Whitehall outside the Banqueting Room, when King Charles I, son of James I, was executed, not by a terrorist's bomb, but with a government-approved axe. This took place on 30 January, the anniversary of the death of four of the plotters at St Paul's churchyard. The significance and symbolism of that would not have been lost on the crowd who gathered to witness the execution of the king.

The fate of the principal characters

Name	Died	Mode of death	Location	Age at death
Thomas Bates	1606	Executed	St Paul's Churchyard	36
Robert Catesby	1605	Shot	Holbeach House	32
Sir Everard Digby	1606	Executed	St Paul's Churchyard	30
Guido Fawkes	1606	Executed	Old Palace Yard Westminster	36
John Grant	1606	Executed	St Paul's Churchyard	36?
Robert Keyes	1606	Executed	Old Palace Yard Westminster	41
Thomas Percy	1605	Shot	Holbeach House	45
Ambrose Rookwood	1606	Executed	Old Palace Yard Westminster	28
Francis Tresham	1605	Poisoned?	Tower of London	38
Robert Wintour	1606	Executed	St Paul's Churchyard	41
Thomas Wintour	1606	Executed	Old Palace Yard Westminster	35
Christopher Wright	1605	Shot	Holbeach House	35
Jack Wright	1605	Shot	Holbeach House	37
Father Henry Garnet	1606	Executed	St Paul's Churchyard	51
James I	1625	Accidental arsenic poisoning?	Theobalds	59
Prince Charles	1649	Beheaded as King Charles I	Whitehall	38

Guy Fawkes' Lantern, now in the Ashmolean Museum

The verdict of history

'The wise inherit honour, but fools he holds up to shame.' Proverbs 3:35

This was a day and an event that would not be forgotten quickly. 'Every year after the gunpowder plot the day was marked by the ringing of church bells, the lighting of bonfires, and special sermons across the land. It was not a holiday as such, but certainly special, an occasion to reflect on God's providence and his mercies to England.'[1] And the effects of that time still resonate into the twenty-first century, for although the cellar where Guy Fawkes stacked the gunpowder was destroyed in the fire that devastated the medieval Houses of Parliament, the Yeoman of the Guard still ritually inspects the cellars before every state opening of Parliament.

The plot, though it made certain the loyalty of the population to the crown, only exacerbated their hatred of Romanism. In reaction to the failed plot, fresh laws were passed that put all Roman Catholics under the iron rule of the government. These included the following:

They were forbidden to appear at Court.

They were forbidden to dwell within ten miles of London.

They were not allowed to remove five miles from their homes, without permission of the neighbouring magistrates.

They were not allowed to become doctors, clerks, lawyers, or members of corporations;

Married Roman Catholics, unless they had been united by a Protestant clergyman, held no legal right to property accruing to either party by marriage.

The houses of Roman Catholics might be broken up and searched, on the order of a single magistrate, at any time, and under any pretext.

Every Protestant, entertaining a Roman Catholic visitor, or employing a Roman Catholic servant, was liable to a heavy fine.

Any Roman Catholic refusing to deny his or her belief in the Holy See became liable to perpetual imprisonment.[2]

In addition to these things, Roman Catholics could not go to university, and they could not become an officer in the army or navy, neither could they stand for Parliament. It was not until 1829 that Roman Catholics were allowed back into Parliament, and it is still against the law for a Roman Catholic to be the King or Queen of England, although this may well change in the future with the current Prince of Wales married to a Roman Catholic.

Harsh as these things undoubtedly were for Bible-believing Christians in Britain and across the world, 1605 was a crucial year for the development of Protestant Christianity, principally because of what did *not* happen. The gunpowder did not ignite and King, Parliament, Bible translators, and the general public were saved not only from immediate extinction, but also great uncertainty, given that the ruling power would have been swept away.

God graciously allowed the opening of Parliament to be put back several times; this caused the gunpowder to deteriorate, thus eliminating the possibility of an explosion. As a result of the failure of the terrorists to succeed in their dreadful scheme, God's people in Great Britain have had a positive effect for the gospel across the world.

Although none can applaud the dreadful sufferings and deaths of the conspirators who were executed in London, many can surely give thanks that the foiling of their plot enabled many positive things to come about since that time, for the cause of Christ.

Think about this

If Parliament had met at the first date, and if the plotters had succeeded in igniting their freshly positioned gunpowder, then there would have been no 1611 King James Bible for it would never have seen the light of day. Undoubtedly, the church and new regime would have sought to undo the damage they thought had been inflicted on it by William Tyndale and his Bible translation, and in its place would have been at best the Douai version. It is amazing that although fifty-four translators on six committees took seven years to bring this version to completion, eighty per cent of the King James Bible is from the pen of William Tyndale!

With there being no new Bible, there would have been no full flowering of the Puritan movement with its vast treasure of godly literature, as their activities would have been curtailed dramatically as a direct consequence.

In all probability, the Pilgrim Fathers would not have been allowed to gather at Southwark in London and then set sail across the Atlantic unmolested to form a new Christian society in North America. As the King James Bible has been the single biggest influence on American life, think about the consequent effect on global history that would have occurred if godly men and women had not been responsible for laying such a good foundation in the New World. Also, the history of the Church across the world would have been drastically affected, for would such a person as Jonathan Edwards, who is possibly the greatest theologian since New Testament times, have risen to such heights to leave such a wonderful example as well as a wealth of profound literature? Or would Princeton Seminary have been founded and been allowed to flourish in such a God-honouring way? Would the great preachers and leaders have been allowed time and space to develop, and would many of the great Bible colleges and missions have been founded? Would the Wycliffe Bible Translators be permitted to have its headquarters in America? Humanly speaking, it is very doubtful if any of these things would have taken place. What a loss that would have been to the global cause of Evangelical, Reformed Christian work.

Back in England, the foiling of the plot saved the nation from following the fate of many other countries where, over the centuries, Roman Catholicism has dominated. It would have become a hard place for the cause of the gospel. The rise of Oliver Cromwell and the Commonwealth would have been prevented, and the extraordinarily popular book by John Bunyan, *The Pilgrim's Progress*, would never have got off the press, especially in the light of his strident comments about the Roman Catholic Church and the Pope.

The Westminster Confession of Faith would never have been produced, as it dealt with the nature of salvation, the church and church government from a Protestant standpoint. The compilers could not have met in the

Jerusalem Chamber to bring such an important work into being, because Westminster Abbey would have been in ruins as a result of the explosion caused by Guy Fawkes. The Congregationalists would not have been able to meet in 1658 to form the Savoy Declaration, and neither would the Baptists have met in 1689 to produce their Confession of Faith.

Notwithstanding the sovereignty of God, it is almost certain that no Protestant revival a century later, under George Whitefield, John and Charles Wesley, Daniel Rowland and their colleagues would have taken place, seeing as so many of them had been influenced for good by Puritan literature. If it hadn't been for the revival, England would probably have followed France into a bloody revolution.

Hymnody would have suffered greatly, too, for the works of Isaac Watts, Charles Wesley and others would not have been allowed to be published and the world would have been all the poorer because no one would ever have been able to sing such majestic hymns.

In all probability, there would have been no Protestant William Carey, and thus no modern missionary movement, which has had so many positive benefits on numerous countries and cultures across the world.

Charles Haddon Spurgeon would not have been influenced so profoundly by *The Pilgrim's Progress* and by many other Puritan works that he not only championed, but also assisted in arranging their republication. Nor would Spurgeon have risen to such prominence in Victorian England and the riches of his magnificent sixty-two volume sermon series would never have been read. Just think how the Christian world would have been impoverished because of such a lack of godly material!

In the twentieth century, Martyn Lloyd-Jones' fresh championing of the Puritans would never have taken place, along with the many fruits of his ministry that came about because of his stand for historic Protestant biblical Christianity, as he led the way in the recovery of expository preaching. Added to this is the work of the Banner of Truth Trust, the International Fellowship of Evangelical Students and the London Theological Seminary, which were all greatly influenced by him. Other publishing houses, like Soli Deo Gloria Publications, would not have had such rich material from the Puritan era, and beyond, to place before the Christian public.

All of these points are just some examples of God's superintending providence, keeping the Gunpowder Plot from being successful.

A view from history

Many years later, the famous Bible commentator, Matthew Henry, preached from Isaiah 51:23 on 5 November 1712, 'Which have said to thy soul, Bow down that we may go over,' under the title, *Popery, A Spiritual tyranny*.

Sometimes God is pleased when he takes the cup of trembling out of the hands of his oppressed people, to put it into the hands of their oppressors that afflicted them; that they may themselves know what it is to be terrified, who have taken a pride and pleasure in terrifying others.

This was fulfilled in the glorious deliverances which we this day celebrate the memorial of. What a cup of trembling was put into the hands of our popish adversaries, when the plot was discovered, and 'those who made the pit, and digged it, fell into the ditch which they made,' Psalm 7:15. And it proved an occasion of putting an edge both upon the laws and upon the spirits of the nation against popery.

We are this day giving God thanks for the deliverance of our land from popery; its first deliverance at the Reformation, when popish errors and delusions were discovered, disowned, and protested against, popish powers shaken off and broken, and popish idolatries and superstitions rooted up and purged out; its many deliverances since, from the restless attempts of those inveterate hereditary enemies of our peace, to bring us back into Egypt again; particularly, its deliverance from that base and barbarous design of blowing up the parliament house with gunpowder this day, 107 years ago; a deliverance never to be forgotten by a people who to this day reap the blessed fruits of it, inasmuch as we should to this day have been groaning under the dismal fatal consequences of the plot, if it had taken effect.[2]

Burn the Robert?

Religious conflicts marked Shakespeare's lifetime. He had been born into a Roman Catholic family, but also was influenced by the Protestant cause, and his writing displays an oppositional stance between both sides. The play, *King Lear*, was written during this time of sensational events. His great Scottish play, *Macbeth*, would have been very different if it were not for the events of 1605, for it included many references to this plot when it appeared in 1606, and acted as a reminder to the population that they had been delivered from tyranny.

The Roman Catholic author, Lady Antonia Fraser, writes fairly of those conspirators: 'The gunpowder plotters were terrorists and they were defeated. They were not good men—by no stretch of the imagination can they be described as that. The study of history can at least represent the plotters as brave bad men; perhaps misguided men is a kinder verdict which may be allowed at this distance of time.'[4]

One consequence of the actions of the conspirators is 'Guy Fawkes Night', with bonfires, fireworks and food, when poor old Guy is normally placed on the top of the fire. Yet even that is an irony of history, because the leader of the plot was Robert Catesby, the Prince of Darkness, and it should be him sitting precariously atop the bonfire. However, it was Guy Fawkes who was caught and who has subsequently caught the imagination of the public, and to be honest, 'Penny for the Robert' does not have the same ring about it. St Peter's school in York, where Guy Fawkes was a pupil, has a bonfire every 5 November, but there is no Guy on it, because it is said that it is bad to burn a former pupil!

In the overthrow of the plot, the Protestant Church has seen God's sovereign overruling and his preserving of the true faith, and the plot's failure certainly changed history. The Puritan Richard Sibbes (1577–1635), preaching on 'The Saints Safety in Evil Times' delivered at St Mary's, Cambridge, on 5 November on occasion of the Powder Plot, published in 1633. His text was Psalm 7:14, 'Behold, he travaileth with iniquity, and hath conceived mischief, and brought forth a lie', and, in giving details of the enemies of God, he said:

Our gunpowder plotters were as pregnant in mischief as ever these. For conception, it could not but come from beneath the vault. There was the very quintessence of devilishness in it. Satan emptied all his bowels, as it were in this project. If all the devils in hell were set awork to devise the like, they could hardly do it. There was scarce from the beginning of the world, a design more prodigious and unmerciful, of greater depth and extent of villainy.

Chapter 10

Were it not for this anniversary commemoration of it, posterity would hardly believe that a plot so hellish could be hatched in the hearts of men, of English men, of Catholic men, as they would be termed, of men borne withal, notwithstanding their dangerous correspondency with foreign enemies, and but half subjects, their better parts, their spirits, being subject to another visible head, who can untie the bond of allegiance at his pleasure.

Neither did they only conceive this hellish wickedness, but were big of it, and kept it close many months, and pleased themselves in the same, as monstrous and misshapen as it was. There wanted neither wit, nor counsel, nor combination, nor secret encouragement to effect it.

Nay, it was an holy villainy, sealed with oaths, sacrament, and all the bonds of secrecy that could be invented. Oh horrible profanation, to set God's seal to Satan's plot. But God, who delighteth to confound all presumptuous attempts, discovered it when it should have come to birth, and so it proved but the untimely fruit of a woman.

They brought forth a lie, for whereas they intended to have blown up king and kingdom, churchman and church, statesmen, yea, the whole state itself, all at once, without warning to prepare themselves for another world, they not only missed of this, but brought ruin upon themselves for another world which they intended to others; whereas they thought for ever to have established their (religion, shall I call it, or idolatry, or) superstition, they have by this means made it more odious than ever before; as the northern gentleman could say, that though he was not able to dispute, yet he had two arguments against popery, equivocation and the gunpowder-treason. But they turn it off easily, as they think. Alas! It was but the plot of a company of unfortunate gentleness. It was our happiness that they were unfortunate; whereas if it had succeeded well, they would have had other terms for it.

Successful villainy goeth for virtue.

Well, the net is broken, and we are delivered. God thought of us when we thought not of him, and awaked for us when we were asleep, (here is a place for behold), for what a miserable face of things would there have been if their plot had succeeded!'5

Humanly speaking, if the plot had succeeded, the king, many of his family, and the majority of Parliament, would all have been blown up, and the forces of darkness would have swept over the land. There should be no doubt about that. Without its discovery and foiling, the history of the world would have been dramatically different, and England would have been plunged into years of uncertainty and great bloodshed.

And there's more

Sixty-three years later, in 1668, the English King James II lost popularity when he became a convert to Roman Catholicism. He had aroused many fears by giving appointments in the army, church and law to those who were Roman Catholics, thus fuelling fears of a forthcoming Catholic tyranny. His opponents sparked off the Glorious Revolution by inviting William III of Orange to claim the throne. So another 5 November became a significant date, for in 1688, William landed at Torbay in Devon, with his army. Along with his wife, Mary, William accepted a Bill of Rights, which curbed Royal Power and restricted succession to the throne to Protestants. This is still the case today.

One unusual result of the plot is that no Member of Parliament can die in the Houses of Parliament. If one does happen to expire in the buildings, the death certificate will have St Thomas Hospital—across the River Thames—as the place of death.

In the Western world, one of the great privileges that have been hard won is the freedom of the press and free speech. Although many deplore the moral decline when it ventures into areas that are less then savoury, freedom of speech (but without abuse) is a wonderful thing. The plotters wanted to eradicate freedom of speech and impose an older and more superstitious way of life on a people who had moved away from such things.

If one thinks about it, the outcome of their actions would have been just as dramatic as if the Nazis had triumphed and overrun Europe in the Second World War with all the concomitant consequences for life in general. So, although we can see the reason why such an audacious plan was hatched, we cannot applaud the motives, any more than we can support those who try to change society today using intimidation, a gun or a bomb.

'I see no reason why gunpowder treason should ever be forgot.'

Although it rarely happens in the twenty-first century, 'Gunpowder sermons became a yearly ritual in Jacobean England. The fifth of November became the day, far more than any anniversary of the Armada, on which God had saved Protestant England from the forces of darkness.'[6]

For Christians in England, then, 1605 should be as well known as 1066, The Battle of Hastings, Martin Luther's nailing of his ninety-five theses in 1517, The Armada of 1588, or The Great Ejection of 1662, because the resultant saving of the cause of Protestant Christianity has brought blessing to countless numbers since that cold November day.

Every year when the anniversary comes around and many fireworks light up the night sky, let all remember and be thankful that God permitted The Powder Treason to fail, so that by contrast the light of his Word might be seen more clearly, and that through its growing influence in the world since 1605, many have turned from their sin to the Saviour of the world.

May all be able to rejoice in the freedom that Christ alone gives to all who love and follow him. Bible-believing Christians should seek to change life for good, not through violence, but through the proclamation of God's Word and by living such lives that honour and glorify his Son, Jesus Christ the Lord.

St Peter's School, York, Guy Fawkes' school

Chapter 1: The big bang
1 **P.G. Wodehouse,** *Service with a Smile*, (Harmondsworth: Penguin), p. 12.
2 **C.H. Spurgeon,** *Metropolitan Tabernacle Pulpit*, Sermon number 2908 (Pasadena, TX: Pilgrim Publications) p. 529,. See also *The C.H. Spurgeon Collection CD-Rom* (Ages Digital Library).
3 **Irving Hexham,** *The Christian Travellers Guide to Great Britain* (Grand Rapids: Zondervan Publishing House), p. 241.
4 **John Flavel,** *The Works of John Flavel*, Volume 4 (London: Banner of Truth Trust), p. 570.

Chapter 2: Conspirators unmasked
1 **Christopher Hill,** *The World Turned Upside Down* (Harmondsworth: Penguin, 1975), p. 40.

Chapter 3: What do you believe?
1. **Brian Edwards,** *God's Outlaw* (Welwyn: Evangelical Press), p. 61.
2. **Simon Schama,** *A History of Britian*, Volume 1 (London: BBC, 2000), p. 238.

Chapter 4: The legacy of history
1 **Michael Wood,** *In Search of England: Journeys into the English Past* (London: Viking), p. 17.
2 **David Daniell,** *William Tyndale* (New Haven: Yale University Press, 1994), p. 78.

Chapter 5: The fiery queen
1 **David Starkey,** *Elizabeth* (London: Vintage, 2001), p. 310.

Chapter 6: A new Bible
1 **J.W.C Wand,** 'Our Faith', in *Our Way of Life* (London: Country Life, 1951), p. 11.
2 **Adam Nicholson,** *Power and Glory, Jacobean England and the Making of the King James Bible* (London: HarperCollins, 2003), p. 112.

Chapter 7: Terrorists plot
1 **Tony Robinson,** *The Worst Jobs in History* (London: Boxtree, 2005), pp. 106,108.

Chapter 8: 5/11
1 **CBBC Newsround** web site.
2 **Adam Hart-Davis,** *What the Tudors & Stuarts Did for Us* (London: Boxtree, 2002), pp. 69–70, for a vivid picture and description of the Scavenger's daughter.

Chapter 9: Unfit to live

1. **Martyn Lloyd-Jones,** Romans Exposition of Chapter 13 Life in Two Kingdoms (Edinburgh: Banner of Truth Trust), p. 61.

Chapter 10: The verdict of history

1 **Alan Haynes,** The Gunpowder Plot (Stroud: Sutton, 2001), p. 136.

2 **Philip Sydney,** A History of the Gunpowder Plot (Protestants Today), p. 126.

3 **Matthew Henry,** The Complete Works of Matthew Henry, treatises, sermons and tracts, Volume 2 (Grand Rapids: Baker Book House), pp. 335,337.

4 **Antonia Fraser,** The Gunpowder Plot, Terror and Faith in 1605 (London: Weidenfeld and Nicoloson, 1996), p. 295.

5 **Richard Sibbes,** Works of Richard Sibbes, Volume 1, (Edinburgh: Banner of Truth Trust), p. 310.

6 **Adam Nicholson,** Power and Glory, Jacobean England and the making of the King James Bible (London: HarperCollins, 2003), p. 110.

D ay One has produced a number of high quality Travel Guides that are suitable for both the armchair as well as the active traveller. They add colour and background to a number of people and places mentioned in this book and come highly recommended.

• Reign of Mary I
  Travel with the Martyrs of Mary Tudor by Andrew Atherstone
• Mary Queen of Scots and James I
  Travel with John Knox by David Campbell
• Puritan life
  Travel with John Bunyan by John Pestell
• William Grimshaw and the spread of Methodism in the North of England
  Travel with William Grimshaw by Fred Perry
• William Carey and the modern missionary movement
  Travel with William Carey by Paul Pease
• Spurgeon and his love of Puritan literature
  Travel with Spurgeon by Clive Anderson
• William Booth and his concern for the needs of ordinary people
  Travel with Booth by Jim Winter
• Martyn Lloyd-Jones and his championing of Puritan literature
  Travel with Martyn Lloyd-Jones by Philip Eveson

For details of future titles in this series, including Oliver Cromwell, Jonathan Edwards, C S Lewis, George Müller, John Newton, John and Charles Wesley, George Whitefield, and William Wilberforce, and details of the Travel Guide Book Club, please contact Day One.